HAUNTED
LONDON

HAUNTED LONDON

RICHARD JONES

Photography by

CHRIS COE

NEW HOLLAND

First published in 2004 by
New Holland Publishers (UK) Ltd
London • Cape Town • Sydney • Auckland

www.newhollandpublishers.com

Garfield House, 86–88 Edgware Road, London W2 2EA,
United Kingdom

80 McKenzie Street, Cape Town 8001, South Africa

14 Aquatic Drive, Frenchs Forest, NSW 2086, Australia

218 Lake Road, Northcote, Auckland, New Zealand

ISBN 1 84330 615 8

Publishing Manager: Jo Hemmings
Project Editor: Camilla MacWhannell
Cover Design and Design: Alan Marshall
Maps: William Smuts
Editor: Sarah Larter
Production: Joan Woodroffe

Reproduction by Pica Digital Pte Ltd, Singapore
Printed and bound by Kyodo Printing Co
(Singapore) Pte Ltd

Page 1: Ye Olde Mitre Tavern, East End
Page 2: Admiralty Building, Westminster
Opposite: Tower of London, East End

CONTENTS

INTRODUCTION

L ONDON HAS THE REPUTATION of being the most haunted capital city in the world. Its ghosts span the centuries and often illuminate dark corners of its brutal past. From those who perished inside England's most haunted building, the Tower of London, to the tragic victims of the world's most famous serial killer, Jack the Ripper, many of the phantoms that roam the capital are an essential part of British history, folklore and legend.

London was founded by the Romans and, since their departure in AD 410, centuries of demolition and rebuilding have seen the level of the city's streets rise by an amazing 28 feet. Millions of people have lived and died in London and, as a consequence, there is not a square inch of the old city that is not imbued with the memories and experiences of these former citizens. There is an old saying that ghosts only ever appear in places that have known either great happiness or great misery, and the buildings and streets of London have certainly known both in abundance. But what exactly are these 'things' that we call ghosts?

The most frequent question I get asked as I go about my business, collecting and researching ghost stories and hauntings, is: 'Do you believe in ghosts?' The answer has to be an emphatic 'yes'. There have, over the centuries, been too many accounts of ghosts and hauntings from honest, reliable and publicity-shy people for them not to exist. I certainly do not believe that they are the dead coming back to haunt the living. Indeed, the more I research and explore supernatural phenomenon – and over the last 20 years I have travelled the length and breadth of Britain and Ireland visiting almost 2,000 haunted places – the more I become convinced that ghosts are little more than strong emotions that have some-how become imprinted upon their surroundings. I also believe that there are certain people who are more attuned to these 'recordings' than the rest of us. This may be why ghosts can be so personal. You might have an entire group of people present when a haunting occurs and yet only a tiny minority of them might be lucky – or unlucky – enough to see the ghost.

Of course, hauntings can assume many different forms. It is, in fact, very rare for people to actually 'see' a ghost. People sense them, smell them, feel them and hear them, but a full-blown manifestation tends to be the exception rather than the rule. In recent years, largely since the advent of digital cameras,

RIGHT: Many a gruesome sight is displayed within the museums of the Royal College of Surgeons, Lincoln's Inn Fields, and you might even bump into the odd ghost.

LEFT: Those who visit the church of St James Garlickhythe may well encounter its mummified ghost 'Jimmy Garlick'.

OPPOSITE: Many a ghostly occurrence has been reported by the gardeners whose job it is to keep the eerie burial ground of Bunhill Fields in good condition.

inter-planetary life forms to view life on Earth and other planets.' Personally I am very dubious about orbs and think there is nothing in the least bit ghostly about the majority of them. As John Mason — a professional photographer who is frequently on the road taking infra-red film and digital images of haunted places — points out, orbs are mostly a product of the digital age. He believes them to be nothing more than light reflecting off particles of dust or moisture in the atmosphere; in other words they are physical rather than psychical objects.

But that aside, ghost stories are as popular now as they have ever been. In the pages that follow you will find a collection of almost 200 of London's most haunted places. Some of the stories are well known and have been handed down through the ages — no doubt they have been embellished with each retelling — while others appear here for the first time in print, and some occurred as recently as June 2003. Although I have tried, wherever possible, to offer historical corrobo-

there has been a sharp increase in the number of supposed ghost photographs, mostly consisting of so-called 'orbs'. These floating balls of circular light are one of the most common types of alleged paranormal activity. Many paranormal investigators enthusiastically hail them as spirit manifestations, and it has been theorized that they may be a kind of spirit energy that is not normally visible to the naked eye, but which can be captured on camera. Some believe them to be spirits that have willingly stayed behind because they feel bound to their previous life or location. One enthusiastic orbist even goes as far as to declare them to be 'multi-dimensional beings' and claims that some of them are '... currently being used by

ration for the events that led to some of the hauntings, I have set the stories down more or less as they were recounted by those who experienced them and I have made few attempts to explain them. I hope that you enjoy the book and that you will take the opportunity to visit some, if not all, of the places included. And, if it should happen that you encounter a ghost, then I would be delighted to hear of your experience.

Richard Jones
South Woodford, London
www.haunted-britain.com

Theatreland & The West End

The ghosts that roam the streets and buildings of London's West End are an eclectic mix. From England's most famous theatre ghost 'The Man in Grey' to the hidden horrors of what was once known as the most haunted house in London, the spectres in this chapter cover all ages and all types. There are also a fair smattering of pubs with ghosts and even an underground station with its very own resident spook.

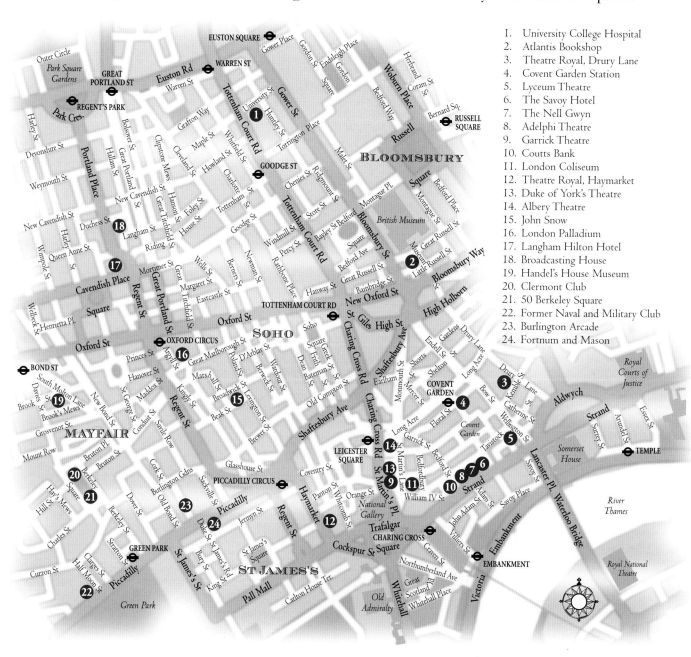

1. University College Hospital
2. Atlantis Bookshop
3. Theatre Royal, Drury Lane
4. Covent Garden Station
5. Lyceum Theatre
6. The Savoy Hotel
7. The Nell Gwyn
8. Adelphi Theatre
9. Garrick Theatre
10. Coutts Bank
11. London Coliseum
12. Theatre Royal, Haymarket
13. Duke of York's Theatre
14. Albery Theatre
15. John Snow
16. London Palladium
17. Langham Hilton Hotel
18. Broadcasting House
19. Handel's House Museum
20. Clermont Club
21. 50 Berkeley Square
22. Former Naval and Military Club
23. Burlington Arcade
24. Fortnum and Mason

THE
OPERA
TAVERN
1879

Krypto

THE OPERA TAVERN

Finest Selection Of Wines   Cask Ales Fro— Wood

MENU

PREVIOUS PAGE: Covent Garden's Opera Tavern is home to a mischievous ghost that has made the lives of several of its managers 'interesting'.

ABOVE: Drury Lane's Theatre Royal, where many ghosts refuse to take a final bow and return to the spotlight time and again.

FORMER UNIVERSITY COLLEGE HOSPITAL
GOWER STREET, WC1
Lizzie's Concerned Spectre

There is a ghostly nurse who makes an occasional appearance at the old University College Hospital building, now part of the college's medical school, but her intentions are all good. She is known as Lizzie, and it is thought that she is the ghost of an early 20th-century nurse who accidentally administered a lethal dose of morphine to a patient. By one of those tragic twists of fate with which the pages of ghostly lore are littered, the patient also happened to be her fiancé. It is said that whenever nurses were about to inject dangerous drugs into a patient Lizzie's watchful wraith would appear to ensure that all went well.

ATLANTIS BOOKSHOP
49A MUSEUM STREET, WC1
The Curious Entity

The Atlantis Bookshop was founded by Michael Houghton in 1922 and has the distinction of being the oldest occult bookshop in London. When the shop's manager, Caroline Wise, took over the premises in 1989, she realized that inexplicable occurrences in the building were not just confined to the pages of the books displayed upon the shelves. On more than one occasion, she caught glimpses of a tall male figure in old-fashioned grey clothing who would come striding towards the back door and proceed to rattle the handle, although he never actually materialized in the shop itself. Caroline formed the opinion that he was the ghost of a former owner, returning to find the cause of the disturbance occasioned by the change of occupation.

THEATRE ROYAL
DRURY LANE, WC2
A Couple of Clowns and the Man in Grey

The Theatre Royal, Drury Lane is the oldest working theatre in London, and although the present building dates from 1812, the first theatre on the site was founded in 1663. In keeping with its antiquity, many phantoms are known to lurk in the wings behind its spectacular cream portico. There is the ghost of Joseph Grimaldi (1778–1837, see also page 38), who in the course of a long and distinguished theatrical career almost single-handedly laid the foundations of the pantomime tradition. The character of the innocent, white-faced rogue that he created became so universally popular that clowns are still known as 'Joeys' in honour of the father of modern clownery. But the exertions of his craft exacted a terrible toll on Grimaldi's health and he was overcome by a crippling disease that forced him to abandon his profession. By 1818 he was destitute, and so a benefit performance was organized at the Theatre Royal. Despite having to be carried onto the stage, and only able to perform seated, Grimaldi had lost none of his magic, and showed himself able to evoke laughter at will. Although he died in 1837, his ghost has returned many

ABOVE: Joseph Grimaldi was the father of modern clownery. His ghost, in the form of a disembodied head with a white face, haunts Drury Lane's Theatre Royal.

times to the Theatre Royal and is renowned for administering a mischievous kick — actors, cleaners, usherettes have all been on the receiving end of his spectral boot as they go about their everyday tasks. One of Grimaldi's final wishes was that his head should be severed from his body prior to burial. This macabre request was apparently carried out, and this might account for the disembodied white face, which has been seen floating around the theatre.

Another comedian to haunt the Theatre Royal is Dan Leno (1861–1904), who was famed both for his clog dancing routine and his portrayal of a pantomime dame. But at the height of his popularity Dan Leno went mad, and he died aged just 43.

His ghost, however, refuses to depart from the spotlights and often returns for an encore. Leno suffered chronic incontinence and used to disguise the resultant odour with perfume. Actors on stage might not see his ghost, but they often detect his invisible presence as his passage is marked by the smell of lavender left hanging in the air. During a performance of *The Pirates of Penzance* in 1981, Nick Bromley, the company manager, was watching in the wings when he was suddenly pushed violently from behind. He turned around but found that there was nobody there. The next night an actress was standing in exactly the same spot when somebody tugged on her wig from behind. She too found nobody there when she turned to investigate. People passing what was once Leno's dressing room have also reported hearing a rhythmic drumming sound emanating from the room. This is believed to be the sound of his ghost rehearsing his famous clog dancing routine over and over again.

But the theatre's most famous ghost is that of the so-called 'Man in Grey', the limping apparition of a young man in a powdered wig, white-ruffed shirt, grey riding cloak and three-cornered hat. He invariably appears during the hours of daylight, and seldom digresses from a timeworn route. He materializes on one side of the upper circle, and crosses to the other side where he astonishes witnesses by melting into the wall. In 1939 more than half the cast of Ivor Novello's *The Dancing Years* were on stage for a photo call, when they witnessed the ghost cross the upper circle and disappear in time-honoured fashion. He has been seen by members of the audience, by famous actors too numerous to mention, by firemen, theatre managers and many other staff at the Theatre Royal. He has sometimes also been seen sitting in the end seat of the fourth row by the central gangway of the upper circle. One morning a cleaner who was new to the theatre and had no knowledge of its ghost, encountered him in this seat at 10 a.m. Thinking he was an actor, she set down her equipment to speak with him, whereupon he vanished. As she looked round for an explanation she noticed the same figure disappearing into the wall to the side of the circle.

The identity of the Man in Grey remains a mystery, although an intriguing discovery during renovations in the 1870s may shed some light onto what caused his ghost to haunt the theatre. As workmen went about their business they broke into a hidden room behind the wall into which the ghost always vanishes. Inside they found the skeleton of a man. It was surrounded by remnants of grey cloth and had a dagger protruding from its rib cage. It has been speculated that the remains were those of a young man who came up to London during the time of Queen Anne. Having won the affections of an actress at the theatre, he was murdered by her actor lover in a fit of jealous rage and his body was subsequently hidden in the secret recess where it lay undiscovered until the Victorian renovation of the theatre.

But whatever the reason behind his haunting, the Man in Grey is a welcome ghost as it is universally acknowledged that he only ever appears at the beginning of a successful run at the theatre. *The King and I*, *South Pacific* and *Oklahoma* are just three of the productions he has endorsed with his presence, and the long running *Miss Saigon* was honoured with an appearance each time there was a change of cast. He is therefore treated with affection rather than fear and his antics, which include pushing performers to positions from where they can deliver their lines to best advantage, have become the stuff of theatrical legend.

ABOVE: William Terris was a matinée idol of the 19th century. His murder in 1897 left his spirit to roam both Covent Garden Station and The Adelphi Theatre.

OPPOSITE: Patrons of the Lyceum Theatre might well enjoy the added bonus of a severed head appearing in their laps!

COVENT GARDEN STATION, WC2
The Man in the Homburg Hat

On Christmas Eve 1955, ticket inspector Jack Hayden was writing up the log at Covent Garden Station, when the door of his office began to rattle violently. Thinking it was a late night reveller lost in the cavernous depths of the station, Hayden called out, 'There's no way through here.' But the rattling grew more violent, and so the irritated inspector leapt to his feet and threw open the door. He found himself face to face with a tall man in a grey suit, wearing tight trousers and a Homburg hat. The man stared at Hayden without speaking. Then he turned, walked towards the stairway and melted into thin air.

Over the next few years, Jack Hayden encountered the same apparition on no fewer than 40 occasions. Nor was he the only member of the station staff to see it. In early 1956 he was in the mess room with station worker Rose Ring, when a loud scream interrupted their break. Moments later, ticket collector Victor Locker burst into the room, shaking with terror and muttering hysterically: 'A man was standing there… it pressed down on my head… it vanished…'

Locker's experience and his subsequent refusal to work at the station prompted London Underground to call in Eric Davey, a committed Spiritualist. A séance was held, during which Victor Locker suddenly cried out, 'Mr Davey it's on you!' Davey later told *The Sunday Dispatch*: 'I got the name Ter- something.' Somebody suggested the name 'Terris' and pictures of the Victorian actor William Terris were brought and shown to both Hayden and Locker. The moment they saw him, they both cried out, 'That's him!'

Terris was murdered outside the Adelphi Theatre on 16th December, 1897 (*see* page 19). His spectral appearances at Covent Garden Station have been explained by the fact that he was a frequent visitor to a baker's shop that previously stood on the site.

'A MAN WAS STANDING THERE… IT PRESSED DOWN ON MY HEAD… IT VANISHED.'

VICTOR LOCKER ENCOUNTERS THE GHOST OF WILLIAM TERRIS

LYCEUM THEATRE
WELLINGTON STREET, WC2
The Severed Head

In the late 19th century the rafters of the Lyceum Theatre, now restored to its original opulent splendour by Lord Lloyd Webber, echoed to the thunderous applause of audiences that had come to marvel at the lavish Shakespearean productions staged here by Henry Irving and Ellen Terry.

One couple, however, got an added bonus with their ticket in the 1880s when they happened to look over the balcony during an interval, and saw the severed head of a man leering up at them from a lady's lap in the stalls below! Their curiosity aroused, they rose from their seats to investigate, but were forced to sit back down when the play resumed. During the second half of the performance they kept looking over the railings, but the lady had a shawl over her lap. When the curtain came down they raced downstairs and observed the lady leaving the theatre. Unfortunately, such was the press of the crowd that they lost her, and were left to ponder on the grisly enigma they had witnessed.

Some years later, the husband happened to visit a house in Yorkshire where, to his surprise, he saw a portrait of a man whose face was identical to that which he and his wife had seen in the lady's lap at the Lyceum. When he asked the owner of the house who the man was, he was told that it was a distant ancestor who had been beheaded for treason, and whose family once owned the land on which the Lyceum stands.

SAVOY HOTEL
STRAND, WC2
Kaspar the Feline Charm

Since it opened in 1889, the Savoy Hotel – which stands on the site of the Plantagenet nobleman John of Gaunt's Savoy Palace – has been synonymous with wealth and privilege.

ABOVE: Book a table for 13 at the Savoy Hotel's restaurant and you will be joined by Kaspar the Cat to ensure that bad luck does not befall you.

The actor Sir Henry Irving (1838–1905) lived here; Edwardian millionaires thought nothing of flooding its courtyard with champagne; the Italian opera singer Enrico Caruso (1873–1921) sang here and Hollywood actress, Mae West (1893–1980), claimed to have held conversations with her mother's ghost in one of its bedrooms.

In 1898 diamond king Joel Woolf held a dinner party at the Savoy, prior to his return to South Africa. It was noted that there were an unlucky 13 people seated at the table, but Woolf dismissed a comment by one of his guests that the first to leave the table would be the first to die. Indeed, he made a point of being the first to rise to his feet and bid his fellow diners good-night. Shortly afterwards he was shot dead in his office in Johannesburg. Fearful that further parties of 13 might be deterred from booking a table, or even worse might suffer a similar fate, the management of the Savoy commissioned a wooden cat to be carved from a single piece of London plane. They named the cat Kaspar, and ever since, should a party of 13 find themselves dining at the Savoy, another place is set at their table. With a white napkin tied around his neck, a resplendent Kaspar is brought to sit with the guests, and a saucer of milk is placed before him!

THE NELL GWYN
BULL INN COURT, WC2
The Phantom Landlord

This tiny, dark and atmospheric pub is tucked down a narrow alley that leads off the Strand. Several customers have commented on feeling a strange coldness that seems to hang in the air to the left of the bar. In 1997, the landlord became most perturbed by the frequency with which a ghostly hand patted him on his back trouser pocket whenever he stood by this section of the counter. Determined to get to the bottom of the invisible revenant's identity, he paid a visit to a medium. The woman had no notion of what business the landlord was in, or even where he lived, but she informed him that she could sense an old man in a cloth cap, who had previously owned his property, and was very pleased with the way he was treating it. She said that should this former resident ever be unhappy about the running of the building, he would stop at nothing to drive away those whom he held responsible. Interestingly in the past decade, several landlords of the Nell Gwyn have attempted to alter the pub's appearance, and all have ended up leaving for unspecified reasons!

ADELPHI THEATRE
STRAND, WC2
The Murdered Actor

On 16th December, 1897, William Terris, a genial, generous and popular actor-manager, arrived at the stage door of the Adelphi Theatre in Maiden Lane for his evening performance in the play *Secret Service*. As he was unlocking the door, Richard Prince, a bit part player to whom Terris had shown some kindness but who had now become insanely jealous of the actor's success, rushed from the shadows and stabbed him. A crowd soon gathered around the dying man, who lay in the arms of his leading lady, Jessica Milward. As he slipped into unconsciousness, Terris whispered his barely audible last words: 'I will be back.'

In 1928, a tourist walking along Maiden Lane encountered a figure dressed in 'old-fashioned, turn of the century clothes'. He was about to make some comment about the man's outdated fashion sense when the figure suddenly vanished into thin air, 'like a bubble bursting'. Later, when shown a picture of William Terris, the tourist immediately recognized him as the man he had seen.

One afternoon in the same year, an actress was resting between performances in her dressing room at the Adelphi, when she was suddenly gripped by the arms, and the chaise lounge on which she lay began to lurch violently from side to side. The next moment a green light appeared over her dressing-room mirror, she heard two loud raps, apparently

ABOVE: Arthur Bourchier made theatrical history when he banned *The Times* drama critic from the Garrick Theatre in 1903. However, his ghost has not yet been banished from the theatre itself.

emanating from behind the glass, and all went quiet. She later discovered that her dressing room was the one that Jessica Milward used to occupy, and that, whenever he passed it, Terris was in the habit of always knocking twice upon her door.

GARRICK THEATRE
CHARING CROSS ROAD, WC2
The Phantom on the Staircase

Designed in 1889 by Walter Emden and C. J. Phipps for W. S. Gilbert of light opera fame, the Garrick Theatre possesses a 'Phantom Staircase' on which the ghost of a former manager, Arthur Bourchier, frequently manifests itself. His tenure at the Garrick lasted from 1900 to 1915, during which time he made his mark on theatreland when he refused to admit the drama critic of *The Times* to a perfor- mance in 1903. Bourchier's ghost has been seen backstage on several occasions after the curtain has fallen and, during a 1990s refurbishment, several builders who were working on the upper levels of the building were startled when he suddenly appeared before them, and fixed them with a stern stare.

COUTTS BANK
STRAND, WC2
Trouble at the Bank

Coutts Bank is the largest of London's private banks whose most illustrious client is Her Majesty, Queen Elizabeth II. In November 1993, the directors took the unusual step of call- ing upon the services of the psychic medium Eddie Burks, in the hope that he would be able to lay to rest the phantom that was making a decided nuisance of itself in the bank's computer room. A bank spokesperson told *The Times* how some staff had reported 'strange happenings... like lights

ABOVE: John Nash's elegant frontage of the Theatre Royal Haymarket. Here Dickens's mistress trod the boards in the mid 19th century and here Dickens's great friend J. B. Buckstone still puts in an occasional spectral appearance.

going on an off… and an apparition, a shadow was how it was described.' One unfortunate woman was most alarmed when the ghost appeared before her minus its head! A séance was duly held in the course of which Burks made contact with the spirit and learnt that it was Thomas Howard, 4th Duke of Norfolk (1538–72). Howard's plot to marry Mary, Queen of Scots (1542–87) and depose Elizabeth I (1533–1603) in her favour, had resulted in his execution. 'I was beheaded on a summer's day,' the dejected duke informed Burks, 'I have held much bitterness and… I must let this go. In the name of God I ask your help… '

Eddie Burks was able to persuade the spirit that the time had come for him to depart and, on 15th November, 1993, a congregation that included the present Duke and Duchess of Norfolk gathered at a nearby Catholic church to say prayers for the repose of his soul. On leaving the service the present duke was asked by a reporter if he was glad that his ancestor was finally at rest. 'Actually,' came the reply, 'I don't believe in ghosts.'

LONDON COLISEUM

ST MARTIN'S LANE, WC2

The Phantom Soldier Takes his Seat

Designed by Frank Matcham in 1904, the Coliseum is London's largest theatre with a seating capacity of 2,558. It is also famed as the first theatre in England to have possessed a revolving stage. The building was once haunted by a ghostly soldier whose last night of leave had, reputedly, been spent attending a play there. On 3rd October, 1918, the man was killed in action and the next night, as the house lights dimmed for the performance, his ghost came strolling down the gangway of the dress circle and

ABOVE: The ghost of a World War I soldier, who was killed in action, has been known to take a seat at the Coliseum.

turned into the second row. However, as people stood to let him pass, the soldier vanished into thin air. For several years after the cessation of hostilities, this spectre appeared frequently at the theatre, just as the curtain was about to rise. But now his shade is little more than a distant memory, and he has not been seen since the 1920s.

THEATRE ROYAL

HAYMARKET, SW1

A Man of the Theatre – Even in Death

John Nash built the graceful and attractive Theatre Royal in 1821, although it saw its most successful period between 1853 and 1878, under the management of John Baldwin Buckstone (1802–79). A popular actor and comedian, Buckstone was a great friend of Charles Dickens (1812–70). Indeed, Dickens once confessed that he had been so moved by Buckstone's performances when he was boy that he had frequently gone home to 'dream of his comicalities'. Although Buckstone died in 1879, his ghost remained as a guiding spirit at the theatre to which he had devoted 25 years of his life. Within a year of his passing, he was seen in the Royal Box, watching a performance intently.

Since then, many illustrious theatrical folk have seen Buckstone's spectral form in sundry parts of the theatre. Donald Sinden saw him whilst playing in *The Heiress* with Ralph Richardson in 1949. As he passed Richardson's dressing room one night, Sinden noticed a man in a long black coat looking out of the window with his back to him. Thinking it was his co-star he called out 'Goodnight Ralph' and continued on his way. It was then that he heard a familiar voice booming from the stage, and realized that Richardson was still performing and could not, therefore, have been in his dressing room.

On other occasions, stage-hands walking past what was once Buckstone's dressing room have clearly heard a voice rehearsing lines. However, on opening the door they have discovered nothing but an empty room. In 1996 the theatre launched a backstage tour, and invited a group of VIP guests to join a rehearsal of the proposed route. An important inclusion was a visit to Buckstone's room, where participants would be treated to anecdotes about the man who had given so much to the theatre. As the dry run began, the stage manager unlocked the room and went off to attend to other business. When the party arrived at Buckstone's room, the guide turned the handle and discovered that the door was locked. The mystified manager returned with the key, but no matter how hard he tried, he was unable to unlock it. Once the tour had departed, however, the door opened easily. Evidently Buckstone was not eager to welcome guests into his former room!

DUKE OF YORK'S THEATRE

ST MARTIN'S LANE, WC2

The Strangler Jacket

Designed in 1892 by Walter Emden for Frank Wyatt and his wife, Violet Melnotte, the Duke of York's theatre was the first to be built on St Martin's Lane. Violet Melnotte later managed the theatre between 1923 and 1928 and one of her first successes was *London Calling*, which was primarily written by Noël Coward. Indeed such is the allure of the theatre that

ABOVE: Who is the red-eyed phantom that patrons and staff have glimpsed at Soho's John Snow pub? A victim of a 19th century cholera epidemic perhaps?

a man attempting to drown a struggling young woman. Eventually the victim's body collapsed, limp and lifeless, and the man proceeded to remove her clothing, including her bolero-style jacket. He then wrapped her corpse in a blanket and carried it away. With such an apparent, sinister heritage, the jacket was considered an unsuitable prop and it was sold on to an American collector of Victoriana. When his wife tried the jacket on, she too experienced the uncomfortable sensation of strangulation. The garment's current whereabouts are unknown.

ALBERY THEATRE
ST MARTIN'S LANE, WC2
Appearing on Stage

Sir Charles Wyndham built the Albery Theatre in 1903, and his ghost is often seen inside the building. During a break from rehearsals, actor Barry Jones was chatting with an actress on the stage when an elegantly attired man with grey, wavy hair strolled towards them. As they moved aside to allow the man to pass, he nodded his thanks. Greatly intrigued by the man's antiquated appearance, Jones watched him cross the stage and saw him turn out of sight. He followed and asked a door attendant if he knew the identity of the man who had just passed by. The attendant was adamant that he had seen no one, and, furthermore, he insisted that there was nobody in the theatre who remotely resembled Jones's description. Bemused, the actor returned to the rehearsal. A short time later, Jones happened upon a portrait of Sir Charles Wyndham, and instantly recognized him as the man he had seen walking across the stage.

Violet has shown a marked reluctance to leave, and her ghost has frequently been seen mingling with first night audiences.

A disturbing series of events at the theatre in the late 1940s have become legendary in both theatrical and paranormal circles. Among the costumes worn in the production *The Queen Came By* was an old bolero-style jacket that acquired a sinister reputation for attempting to strangle any actress who wore it. No matter how much it was let out, actresses would complain that the garment started to shrink the moment they put it on, growing tighter and tighter around them. In an attempt to solve the mystery of what lay behind the phenomenon, a séance was held and one of the mediums present clearly saw

JOHN SNOW
BROADWICK STREET, W1
The Phantom with the Blood Red Eyes

The John Snow public house is named for John Snow (1813–58), the doctor who saved the lives of thousands of Londoners by proving that cholera was a water-borne disease. Quite who haunts the pub is not known, but several managers have reported feeling an invisible, icy presence brushing past them as they count the takings at the end of the day. Several

ABOVE: Today, the rafters of the London Palladium may well resound with laughter and cheers, but its ghost belongs to a bygone age.

customers have also recounted spotting a shadowy figure sitting in the corner of the bar, its face twisted into a horrible, pain-racked grimace and its ghastly red eyes staring into space. It has been speculated that it might be the ghost of one of the unfortunate victims of the cholera epidemic, which devastated the surrounding Soho streets in 1854.

LONDON PALLADIUM
ARGYLL STREET, W1
The Spectral Lady in the Crinoline Dress

Opened in 1910 as the Palladium Music Hall, this luxurious theatre became the London Palladium in 1934. It was during a television interview in March 1973 that a doorman gave the first hint of something otherworldly roaming the theatre. The building's ghostly presence has a penchant for the old Crimson Staircase located at the rear of the Royal Circle and which is believed to be a remnant of Argyll House, which stood on the site until 1864. A spectral lady in a crinoline dress has been seen gliding up and down the staircase by a number of people, including usherettes, theatre hands and visiting artistes.

Nobody knows who the woman is, although it has been suggested that she might be Mrs Shireburn, mistress of the Duke of Argyll, who lived in Argyll House between 1750 and 1762, and to whom he left his entire property in England.

LANGHAM HILTON HOTEL
PORTLAND PLACE, W1
The Thing in Room 333

A forerunner of London's grand hotels, the Langham Hotel was built in 1864. Its Victorian splendour was host to such famous names as Mark Twain, Arnold Bennett, Napoleon III of France, and the composer Dvorák — who managed to offend the sensibilities of the management when, in an attempt to save money, he requested a double room for himself and his grown up daughter.

But as even grander hotels were built across London, the Langham's popularity waned, and by the 1950s it had been pressed into service as administrative offices for the BBC, whose radio studios still stand opposite. Several rooms on the third floor were maintained as accommodation for staff whose early starts or late finishes necessitated an overnight stay. One night in 1973, announcer James Alexander Gordon was sleeping in room 333 when he awoke to find a fluorescent ball hovering on the opposite side of the room. As he watched, it began to take on the clearly defined form of an Edwardian gentleman in full evening dress. Summoning up all his courage, the terrified presenter asked who the apparition was and what it wanted. The question seemed to irritate the phantom, for it began to come towards him, its arms outstretched, its eyes fixed and unblinking. Unable to take any more Gordon rushed from the room and raced down to the commissionaire who was not in the least bit sympathetic and refused point blank to accompany him back to the room. Gordon returned to room 333 alone, and found his mysterious guest still present, although its appearance seemed less distinct than it had been. Later, when he told his colleagues at Broadcasting House about his ordeal, others told of encountering the apparition in that same bedroom.

The building has now been completely renovated and once more functions as a luxury hotel. However, ghostly activity continues in room 333. In May 2003, a woman staying in the room checked out of the hotel suddenly, without giving any reason for her premature departure. A few days later she sent a letter explaining that her slumbers had been interrupted by the activities of the ghost that kept her awake by repeatedly shaking the bed during the night.

OPPOSITE: When the Handel House Trust acquired the former home of the composer, a ghostly presence was included at no extra cost!

BELOW: Although Room 333 at The Langham Hilton has now been transformed, its resident wraith is still known to chill the blood of the occasional overnight guest.

BROADCASTING HOUSE
PORTLAND PLACE, W1
The BBC's Gaggle of Ghosts

Built to house 22 soundproof studios for the BBC, Broadcasting House has remained relatively unaltered since it opened on 2nd May, 1932. In 1937 the ghostly figure of a man with fine twirling whiskers and dressed in old-fashioned clothes was seen limping around the fourth floor of the building. So real did he look that members of staff mistook him for a senior member of the management until, to their astonishment, he began to dissolve before their eyes. A spectral waiter has also been seen wandering along the corridors of the building, whilst a phantom musician, who appears to be lost, has left behind many a bemused witness, when he has responded to their offer of directions by shaking his head and vanishing!

HANDEL'S HOUSE MUSEUM
25 BROOK STREET, MAYFAIR, W1
The Female Entity That Came to Stay

George Frideric Handel (1685–1759) was 38 years old in the summer of 1723 when he moved into a newly built house at what is now 25 Brook Street. He lived there for 36 years, and died in the upstairs bedroom. In 2000, the upper storeys of the building were leased to the Handel House Trust and on 8th November, 2001, 'Handel's spirit was brought back… when the Handel House Museum opened to the public.'

However, it was reported that a spirit of a very ethereal kind was also haunting the building during the restoration project. In July 2001, the Handel House Trust went as far as to call upon the services of a local priest to see if he could lay to rest the ghost that had been seen by at least two people. 'We weren't sure whether having a ghost would attract or deter customers,' commented Martin Egglestone, a trust fundraiser, who twice encountered the apparition in the room where Handel died. In June 2001, he was helping measure up for some curtains when 'suddenly the air got very thick'. The next moment, a shape that resembled 'the imprint on the back of your retina when you close your eyes, having been looking at the sun for too long' appeared before him. Mr Egglestone described the apparition as female and slightly higher than him. He observed how 'there was no malevolent feeling. It felt like the pressure you get when you brush past someone in the Tube and they are too close to you.'

Staff also reported the strong, lingering scent of perfume hanging in the air of the bedroom. Although Handel lived here alone but for his manservant, he was visited by two sopranos,

Faustina Bordoni and Francesca Cuzzoni. The two singers vied with each other to perform in the composer's operas and Mr Egglestone raised the possibility that the ghost might be one of them. Interestingly, the upper floors of number 23 next door, which are also part of the museum and used for changing exhibitions, were the home of rock legend Jimi Hendrix between 1968 and 1969. He also claimed to have seen a ghost on the premises whilst he lived there. Commenting on the most recent haunting a local priest told The *Daily Telegraph*: 'This is a soul who is restless and not at home. I don't see it as evil or horrible and one should help it to be at peace.'

CLERMONT CLUB
44 BERKELEY SQUARE, W1
The Spectral Servant That Cannot Leave

The writer and historian Nikolaus Pevsner (1902–83) described 44 Berkeley Square as 'the finest terrace house of London'; whilst Horace Walpole, who was a frequent visitor, applauded the building's staircase as being '... as beautiful a piece of scenery and, considering the space, of art as can be imagined... ' The house was designed in 1742 by William Kent for Lady Isabella Finch, a maid of honour to George II's sister, Princess Amelia. Behind its elegant Palladian façade, which fronts an interior of breathtaking splendour, Lady Isabella entertained many luminaries of her age, the proceedings and servants being watched over by her devoted major-domo, who cut a dashing figure in his green livery and powdered wig.

Lord Clermont subsequently bought the house and frequently entertained the Prince Regent, the future George IV (1762–1830), here. Having passed through a succession of owners, in 1959 the Clermont Club took over occupancy. But Lady Isabella's major-domo has chosen to linger on in spirit form. Over the last two centuries, his ghost, resplendent in smart green uniform and handsome periwig, has often been seen flitting up and down the grand staircase, keeping a watchful eye on the playing of roulette and backgammon, which now goes on in the grand salon. The major-domo is said to walk with a slight limp, and his appearances are brief, for having satisfied himself that all is well, he melts through one of the staircase doors and ascends the narrow, spiral staircase to his bedroom at the top of the house.

> '**RUSHING UPSTAIRS, THE FRIENDS THREW OPEN THE DOOR AND FOUND THEIR COMPANION RIGID WITH TERROR, HIS EYES BULGING FROM THEIR SOCKETS...**'

THE MEN WHO CONFRONTED THE BEAST OF BERKELEY SQUARE

50 BERKELEY SQUARE, W1
The Most Haunted House in London!

The plain Georgian exterior of 50 Berkeley Square conceals an interior that still retains much of its 18th-century grandeur. Sweeping staircases, high plaster ceilings, grand over-mantle mirrors, and marble floors and fireplaces, lend the building a decidedly Dickensian air. For over 50 years the house has been the premises of the antiquarian booksellers Maggs Bros, and the ceiling-high rows of heavy mahogany bookcases that line the walls are stacked with shelf after shelf of leather-bound tomes by long-dead men of letters – some famous, many forgotten. Yet there is nothing in the yellowed pages of the thousands of books on display that comes close to matching the sinister happenings that were once an everyday occurrence within these walls. These happenings were so terrifying that for much of the 19th century 50 Berkeley Square was known simply as 'the most haunted house in London'.

Charles Harper in *Haunted Houses* (1907) stated that '... it seems that a Something or Other, very terrible indeed, haunts or did haunt a particular room. This unnamed Raw Head and Bloody Bones, or whatever it is, has been sufficiently awful to have caused the death, in convulsions, of at least two foolhardy persons who have dared to sleep in that chamber... ' One of these persons was a nobleman who scoffed at tales that a hideous entity was residing within the haunted room and vowed to spend the night there. It was agreed, however, that he would ring the servants' bell to summon his friends if he required assistance. So saying, he retired for the night. A little after midnight there was a faint ring, which was followed by a ferocious pealing of the bell. Rushing upstairs, the friends threw open the door and found their companion rigid with terror, his eyes bulging from their sockets. He was unable to tell them what he had seen, and such was the shock to his system that he died shortly afterwards.

As a result of its dreadful reputation, no tenant could be found who was willing to take on the lease of 'the house' in Berkeley Square, and for many years it remained empty. But its otherworldly inhabitants continued to be active: strange lights flashed in the windows and startled passers-by; disembodied screams were heard echoing from the depths of the building and, spookier still, the sound of a heavy body was heard being dragged down the staircase.

OPPOSITE: Although ghosts still wander the cosy interior of 50 Berkeley Square, they are nowhere near as malevolent as they were in the late 19th century when their antics gave the building a truly sinister reputation.

ABOVE: A man ascending the stairs at 50 Berkeley Square once had his glasses snatched from him by an unseen hand. You have been warned!

One night, two sailors on shore leave in London were seeking a place to stay, and chanced upon the obviously empty house. The pair broke in and made their way upstairs, where they inadvertently settled down to spend the night in the haunted room. They were woken by the sound of heavy, determined footsteps coming up the stairs. Suddenly the door banged open and a hideous, shapeless, oozing mass began to fill the room. One sailor managed to struggle past the thing and escape. Returning to the house with a policeman, he found his friend's corpse impaled on the railings outside, his twisted face and bulging eyes a grim testimony to the terror that had caused him to jump to his death, rather than confront the evil that had entered the room.

Many theories have been put forward to account for the haunting of 50 Berkeley Square. Charles Harper reported that the house had once belonged to a Mr Du Pré of Wilton Park who locked his lunatic brother in one of the attics. The captive was so violent that he could only be fed through a hole in the door, and his groans and cries could be heard in the neighbouring houses. When the madman died, his spectre remained behind to chill the blood and turn the mind of anyone unfortunate enough to encounter it. Another hypothesis holds that a Mr Myers, who was engaged to a society beauty, once owned the house. He had set about furnishing the building in preparation for their new life together when, on the day of the wedding, his fiancée jilted him. The disappointment undermined his reason, turning him into a bitter recluse. He locked himself away in the upstairs room and only came out at night to wander the house by flickering candlelight. It was these nocturnal ramblings that, so the theory goes, gave the house its haunted reputation.

Whatever the events, tragic or otherwise, that lie behind the haunting of 50 Berkeley Square, there is no doubt that the building has a definite atmosphere about it. Indeed, it is said that the fabric is so charged with psychic energy that merely touching the external brickwork can give a mild shock to the psychically inclined. Nor, as is often claimed, are the ghosts consigned to the building's past. One Saturday morning in 2001, Julian Wilson, a bookseller with Maggs Brothers, was working alone in the accounts department, which now occupies the haunted room. Suddenly, a column of brown mist moved quickly across the room and vanished. That same year a cleaner preparing the house for a party felt the overwhelming sensation that someone — or something — was standing behind her. Turning around she discovered that the room was empty. Another man was shocked when his glasses were snatched from his hand and flung to the ground as he was walking up the stairs.

In October 2001, I was asked to appear in a BBC documentary about haunted London, and we were fortunate enough to film inside 50 Berkeley Square. Part of the programme entailed the soundman and myself standing within the darkened, haunted room for about five minutes, waiting for the signal to switch the lights on. Although nothing actually happened, I can honestly say that I found it a truly frightening experience, and we were both glad to get out of the room and join the rest of the crew outside.

FORMER NAVAL AND MILITARY CLUB
94 PICCADILLY, W1
Perky Makes His Presence Known

Universally known, from its bold lettering on its stone gateposts, as the In and Out Club, the building that, prior to their recent move to St James's Square, housed the Naval and Military Club, was once, fittingly, the home of Lord Palmerston, whose policy of gunboat diplomacy helped make the British Empire internationally respected in the 19th century. The club was bombed in World War II and two members were killed. One of them, Major Henry Braddell, known as 'Perky', was said to haunt the club's Egremont Room dressed in smart military uniform and ankle-length great coat. Another spectre of unknown gender has been seen elsewhere in the building and has the unnerving habit of suddenly appearing from nowhere and scaring its victims witless! Indeed, many years ago, when a man suddenly went into convulsions and died of a seizure shortly after visiting the club, it was widely rumoured that his fatal fit had been brought on by an encounter with the ghost.

BURLINGTON ARCADE
PICCADILLY, W1
Percy the Poltergeist

Samuel Ware designed Burlington Arcade for Lord George Cavendish in 1819, reputedly to prevent passers-by throwing oyster shells and other rubbish over the wall of his lordship's home next door, Burlington House. The arcade is still patrolled by top-hatted beadles, whose job it is to enforce Regency laws that still forbid shoppers to sing, whistle or hurry. In the 1970s a leather-goods shop in the arcade was plagued by the nocturnal activities of a poltergeist that staff came to know affectionately as 'Percy'. It would seem that objects were lifted off the shelves in the middle of the night to be found the next morning arranged in neat semi-circles upon the floor. Scotland Yard detectives, having eliminated the possibility of human involvement, found themselves at a loss to explain the phenomena. Meanwhile, the management of the shop, spotting the opportunity to enjoy some amusing publicity, placed a sign in the window announcing: 'Poltergeists Gladly Served without Fear or Favour'. This seemed to curb Percy's appetite for mayhem, and shortly afterwards his disturbances ceased and have not been repeated since.

FORTNUM AND MASON
181 PICCADILLY, W1
The Fare Dodging Spectre of Lady C——

In the early 1960s, broadcaster and journalist Nancy Spain was standing outside the main entrance of Fortnum and Mason, attempting to hail a taxi to take her to an important

ABOVE: Burlington Arcade where patrons are expressly forbidden to sing, whistle or hurry. This didn't deter a poltergeist from making a decided nuisance of itself here in the 1970s.

appointment. Every cab that drove by was occupied and she became concerned that she would be late for her meeting. However a taxi then stopped alongside her, and a red-haired old lady climbed out and proceeded to search frantically in her purse for the fare. Desperate to be on her way, Nancy Spain eventually stepped forward and paid for the old lady herself. Thanking her for her kindness, the woman hurried into the shop. As Nancy settled back into the cab en route to her appointment, the driver could not conceal his mirth. 'You was caught there luv,' he told her. 'That was old Lady C—, she hates paying her own fare, but she could buy and sell both of us.' As it happened Nancy Spain was quite amused by the incident. The next day she went to visit her mother, whom she told of her encounter with the miserly aristocrat. Nancy's mother remained strangely silent. Rising from her chair, she picked up a newspaper dated three days earlier and pointed to a headline that read 'LADY C____ DIES IN A FIRE'.

CLERKENWELL TO EMBANKMENT

For centuries Clerkenwell, sitting on the banks of the underground River Fleet, included London's most infamous ghettos and was a place to be avoided. Today, straying into the back streets of Holborn brings you into some wonderfully atmospheric places, like Lincoln's Inn Fields where the ghostly vestiges of past executions drift on the night breezes. By contrast, Temple is a gas-lit oasis from which many former residents are loath to depart.

1. Dickens House Museum
2. Red Lion Square
3. The Dolphin Tavern
4. The Ship Tavern
5. Lincoln's Inn Fields
6. Lincoln's Inn
7. Somerset House
8. Aldwych Station
9. The George
10. Wig and Pen Club
11. Temple
12. Ye Olde Cock Tavern
13. Ye Olde Mitre Tavern
14. Sadler's Wells Theatre

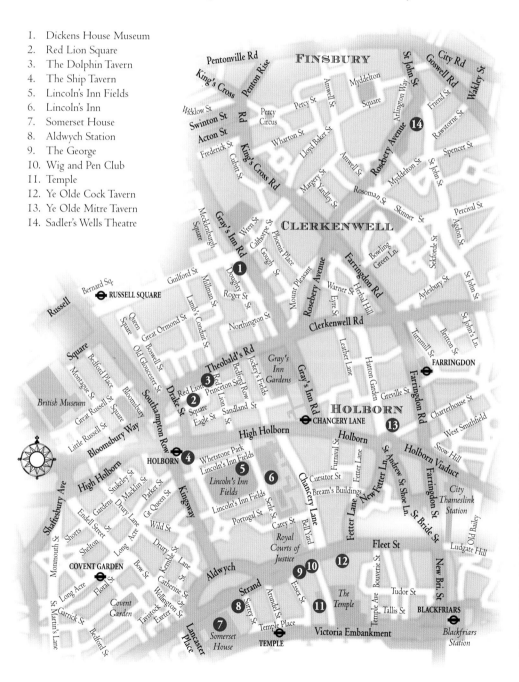

DICKENS HOUSE MUSEUM
48 DOUGHTY STREET, WC1
Dickens Returns

Dickens moved to Doughty Street in March 1837, just as he was starting to find literary success. Whilst living here he finished *The Pickwick Papers*, wrote *Oliver Twist* and *Nicholas Nickleby* and began work on *Barnaby Rudge*. By the time he moved out in December 1839, Dickens was famous throughout the world.

In 1922, the Dickens Fellowship rescued the house from demolition, opening it up to the public a few years later. It is now a treasure trove of relics and articles that depict the great author's life and times. Dickens's ghost appears to relish the pull of the only one of his London homes to have survived and he has been seen on many occasions. One former curator claimed that she frequently saw his distinctive figure bounding enthusiastically along the hallway and up the staircase. In 1972, a group of builders working on an adjacent property saw him glide past them on the pavement outside, turn up the steps of his old home and promptly disappear into the solid front door. One of the workmen is said to have been so affected by the experience that he resigned on the spot and never even went back to collect his wage packet!

BELOW: The Gothic splendour of Lincoln's Inn New Hall stands on the threshold of a true time-capsule where, in the 18th century, Robert Perceval once had an alarming encounter with his own ghost.

RED LION SQUARE, WC1
The Ghostly Regicides

The huge trees that tower over the centre of Red Lion Square cast it into almost perpetual shadow, and it comes as no surprise to learn that the place is haunted. In 1660 Charles II returned from exile in the Netherlands and the Restoration of the monarchy began. Those who had remained loyal to the Royalist cause could look forward to rewards, while those who had supported the Parliamentarian campaign and had welcomed the rule of the Common-wealth under Oliver Cromwell, could expect retribution now that a Stuart sat upon the throne of England again. But the three leading Parliamentarians, Oliver Cromwell, John Bradshaw and Henry Ireton were beyond the King's reach, for they lay buried in the hallowed earth of Westminster Abbey. Not willing to let a little thing like death stand in his way, Charles demanded vengeance and, on 29th January, 1661, the cadavers of the three men were exhumed and put on trial for regicide. Though the men had cheated the axe in life, they would not do so in death. Found guilty they were sentenced to a public beheading at Tyburn. The bodies of Cromwell and Ireton were brought to the Red Lion Inn, which then stood on the site of the square. They remained there overnight, and at dawn the next day, they were taken to Tyburn where, having been joined by the putrefied corpse of Bradshaw, they were hanged by their necks until late afternoon. Cut down, their heads were hacked off and placed on spikes above Westminster Hall, while their bodies were buried in a deep pit beneath the gallows. (See also page 86).

Their ghosts have returned to haunt Red Lion Square on many occasions since. Complete in body, the three men appear to be involved in a deep and animated conversation as they stroll pur-posefully across the square. Once

they arrive in the middle, their revenants become blurry and, with each ghostly step thereafter, they become more and more indistinct until they melt away completely.

THE DOLPHIN TAVERN
44 RED LION STREET, WC1
When Death Rained Down

The Dolphin Tavern is very much a locals' pub and boasts an interior that is functional rather than fashion-able. However, on one of its walls you can see a battered old clock, the hands of which are frozen at 10.40 p.m., much as they have been for almost 90 years. It was at this precise moment, on 9th September, 1915, that a Zeppelin bomb crashed onto the pub and reduced it to a smouldering heap of twisted rubble. Three customers were killed and several others were seriously injured in the tragedy. The clock was dragged from the ruins, and when the pub was rebuilt, it was placed on the wall as a per-manent memorial to that long ago night when death and destruction rained down from above. And, every so often, as the staff are tidying up after another day's trading, their attention is drawn inexplicably to the clock. As they gaze upon its face, they hear a tuneless, mournful whistling that gets lower and lower, until all is quiet once more.

ABOVE: Henry Ireton, along with Oliver Cromwell, undertakes nocturnal spectral rambles across Holborn's Red Lion Square.

LEFT: The hands of the Dolphin Tavern's battered old clock remain eerily frozen at the moment in 1915 when death and destruction rained from the sky.

THE SHIP TAVERN
12 GATE STREET, WC2
The Fugitives' Hideaway

During the despotic reign of Henry VIII, Catholics would sneak to the building that once stood on the site that is now occupied by this cosy 18th-century hostelry to attend mass, conducted by outlawed priests. Lookouts would be posted around the neighbourhood, and a pre-arranged signal would warn the congregation when the king's zealous officials came into view. The warning would, hopefully, give the priest time to escape into one of the pub's several 'hidey-holes', and allow the congregation time to take up their tankards and become just another group of regulars.

Listening as the king's officers searched for them, knowing that discovery would mean imprisonment, torture and certain death, those brave priests must have been quaking with fear; and the feeling of relief, when the officials had departed, and they were able to creep from their hiding places, must have been immense. It is this aura of relief that pervades the atmosphere of the pub, and the staff are extremely fond of their 'happy' ghost. He never actually shows himself, but makes his presence known with his mischievous pranks, such as hiding cooking utensils for a few days, or moving cellar keys to other parts of the pub.

LINCOLN'S INN FIELDS, WC2
The Ghostly Screams That Never Die

Lincoln's Inn Fields evolved from two 'waste common fields', Purse Field and Cup Field. Although it is now the largest square in London, surrounded by an eclectic and elegant mix of buildings and houses of all styles and from all ages, there was a time when it was used as a place of public execution. In 1586, Anthony Babington and his 13 co-conspirators in a plot to assassinate Elizabeth I and put Mary, Queen of Scots onto the throne, were hanged, drawn and quartered in the fields over a period of two days; seven were executed on one day, the remaining six on the next. Babington was still conscious when eviscerated, and endured unimaginable agonies as his comrades looked on knowing that they would soon suffer a similar fate. When Elizabeth heard of his suffering she decided on leniency and the remaining conspirators were shown the mercy of being hanged until dead before disembowelling commenced.

BELOW: Enjoy the hospitality of the Ship Tavern and you may well encounter the happy spectre that roams the pub.

Another to be executed here was William, Lord Russell who was sentenced to death in 1683 for plotting against the life of Charles II. His wife, Lady Rachel Russell, pleaded long and eloquently with Charles to spare her husband's life. The king, however, would not be moved. 'If I do not kill him,' he observed wryly, 'then he will soon kill me.' So it was that Lord Russell strolled bravely to his death, stoically maintaining that the pain of the axe would last for but a moment and cause 'less pain than the drawing of a tooth'. Unfortunately, the notorious and bungling Jack Ketch was wielding the axe, and according to the diarist John Evelyn, it 'took three butcherly strokes' to remove 'the patriot's head.' Ketch later defended his crass ineptitude with the claim, 'his lordship moved!' With such a brutal and barbaric past, it is inevitable that ghosts aplenty wander Lincoln's Inn Fields during the hours of darkness. The apparition of a shadowy, dark, figure has startled several people walking through the square at night. Its nebulous drifting is nearly always accompanied by the sound of pain-racked screams that are carried upon the night breezes.

LINCOLN'S INN, WC2
That's me in the Corner

Lincoln's Inn is one of London's four Inns of Court, societies to which England's barristers and aspiring barristers must belong. It is a tranquil oasis, hidden away from the bustle of modern London and has a timeless, almost antiquated feel about it. In the 18th century, Robert Perceval – cousin of Spencer Perceval (1762–1812), the only British Prime Minister ever to have been assassinated – came to read law at Lincoln's Inn. However, he neglected his studies in favour of more hedonistic pursuits and fell into a thoroughly dissolute lifestyle.

One night, however, he took a break from his usual nocturnal activities of drinking, gambling and whoring, and was, unusually for him, actually studying in his chamber at Lincoln's Inn. As midnight approached, he started to grow a trifle uneasy. When the bell began to chime the hour, a cold shiver suddenly ran down his spine and, turning from his books, he saw a shrouded figure standing behind him. He demanded to know its identity and purpose, but the figure made no reply. Leaping to his feet, Perceval drew his sword, and lurched at his mysterious visitor only to be astonished when the blade passed right through it. Dropping his weapon, he pulled the shroud away from spectre's face and was horrified to find himself face to face with his own image, but with gaping wounds about the face and chest. He stood and stared as his doppelgänger shimmered and melted away slowly. Taking this as a warning that he must mend his ways, Perceval became a reformed character, and, for a time at least, he applied himself rigorously to his studies.

But he soon tired of this, and gradually Perceval slipped back into his old routine, making up for lost time by running up huge gambling debts. One morning his corpse was found

ABOVE: Ghostly moans and agonized cries have been known to shatter the stillness of Lincoln's Inn Fields in the dead of night.

sprawled in a gutter on the nearby Strand. He had been run through with his own sword, and it was noted by those whom he had told of his strange encounter in Lincoln's Inn, that his horrific injuries were more or less identical to those he had seen upon the body of the apparition.

SOMERSET HOUSE
STRAND, WC2
The Heroic Spectre

Somerset House is so-named as it stands on a site formerly occupied by the first Renaissance palace in England, which was built between 1547 and 1550 for Lord Protector Somerset. The current building dates from 1775 and was designed by the architect Sir William Chambers. The buildings that surround its inner courtyard were formerly home to various Admiralty offices. Lord Horatio Nelson (1758–1805) was a frequent visitor to Somerset House, and came here to receive his orders to engage Napoleon's forces at Trafalgar. Having achieved victory, he was fatally wounded in his moment of triumph. Nelson's glowing, though feeble, form has sometimes been seen almost skipping across the courtyard of Somerset House on bright summer's mornings. An empty sleeve swings by his general public departed from the station on the evening of 30th September, 1994. Today, the station is maintained by London Underground, primarily as a museum piece and film set, whilst the ticket hall is frequently rented out for art exhibitions, book launches and other private parties. It is without doubt the most used of the Underground's disused stations and numerous films and television programmes have been shot in its cavernous depths.

Aldwych Station stands on the site of the Royal Strand Theatre, which was demolished in 1905. This may account for the ghostly actress who is often seen strolling along the tracks at night. Indeed, the 'fluffers' – those whose job it is to clean the underground's tunnels and stations at night – have often encountered her melancholic shade, and several of them have, reportedly, been absolutely terrified by the experience.

THE GEORGE
213 STRAND, WC2
The Handsome Phantom

ABOVE: Phantom footsteps have been known to disturb the rest of those spending a night at the 17th-century Wig and Pen Club.

side, and a wispy, transparent cloud hovers above his head. But should anyone approach him, he vanishes in a puff of smoke.

ALDWYCH STATION
STRAND, WC2
The Ghost Line

Aldwych Station opened on 30th November, 1907, and for the next 87 years ran a shuttle service back and forth to Holborn Underground Station. The last train carrying the

Although the current black-and-white timbered frontage of The George pub dates from the 1930s, it stands on much older foundations and is the haunt of a ghost of 17th-century origin. One morning during a refurbishment in the 1970s, a gang of painters and decorators arrived to begin work at the pub. Having allotted various tasks to his men, the foreman went down into the old cellar and set about whitewashing its walls. After about 20 minutes he came racing back upstairs. 'That feller down there, gu'vnor,' the terrified decorator panted to the landlord, 'he just looked at me, didn't say nothin', just stared.' The landlord calmed him down with a glass of brandy and then asked him what the man had looked like. 'All 'istorical like them Roundheads and Cavaliers,' came the breathless reply. The landlord nodded. 'Oh I shouldn't worry about him,' he reassured the unfortunate workman. 'That's just the ghost. My wife sees him all the time.' Quite who he is, or was, nobody has been able to ascertain, but there is a long tradition of his handsome phantom appearing to startled witnesses in the cellar of The George.

WIG AND PEN CLUB
229–230 STRAND, WC2
Ghostly Footfall

The building occupied by the Wig and Pen Club, a club intended for lawyers (the wig) and journalists (the pen), dates from 1625. In the early hours of some mornings an unseen man has been heard pacing along a ground floor corridor by staff staying overnight on the premises. The footsteps have also been heard on some Saturday afternoons. Although no one knows for certain the identity of the invisible phantom, there is a long held tradition that he is the ghost of an overworked solicitor who was found dead in his office that once occupied the premises.

TEMPLE, EC4
The Judge Goes By

The quiet, cloister-like Middle and Inner Temples comprise two of London's four Inns of Court, amongst the timeless alleyways and courtyards of which, barristers — the wigged and robed advocates of the legal profession — have their chambers. It is a tranquil area that time and progress have left untouched, and its enchantment is at its most magical on dark winter nights, when the flickering glow of gaslight casts eerie shadows upon buildings that seem almost marooned in a bygone age. It is on such nights that the Temple's resident wraith stirs from his eternal slumber and hurries once more through places he knew well in life.

Henry Hawkins (1817–1907) was one of the 19th century's most respected advocates. He was called to the bar in 1843 at the age of 26 and spent the rest of his illustrious career in

ABOVE: Arthur Orton arrives at Court. Henry Hawkins successfully disproved Orton's claim to be Roger Tichborne, a man of title and fortune who was, in fact, lost at sea.

and around the Temple. His most famous case was that of the Tichborne Claimant in 1873, when he appeared for the prosecution against Arthur Orton, an Australian butcher who claimed to be Roger Tichborne, heir to a vast fortune and title. The complex case dragged on for 188 days and was, at the time, the longest criminal trial in history. At the end of the trial Orton was found guilty of perjury and sentenced to 14 years' imprisonment. Following this sensational trial Hawkins was made a judge, and in 1899 he was created Baron Brampton.

So attached was Hawkins to the machinations and traditions of his chosen profession that his ghost has proved singularly unwilling to depart from the gas-lit oasis where he made his name. He appears in the hours after midnight, wigged and robed and with a mass of dusty legal papers clutched in his arms. Witnesses can only look on as his shimmering figure races past them at a brisk pace. And as he does so, his image begins to fade until, after just a few tantalizing moments, he dissolves into the night and returns to the realm from whence he came.

YE OLDE COCK TAVERN
22 FLEET STREET, EC4
Oliver Goldsmith's Macabre Meanderings

Dating back to the mid-16th century, Ye Olde Cock Tavern is Fleet Street's oldest pub. It stood on the opposite side of the road originally, but moved to its current location in the early 19th century. Past patrons have included Samuel Pepys and the poet Alfred, Lord Tennyson (1809–92), who once composed a poem to the pub's head waiter. The pub is haunted by the writer Oliver Goldsmith (c. 1730–74) who is buried in Temple Churchyard to the rear of the estab-lishment. One night in September 1984, an Australian barmaid was given the task of taking out the rubbish, which was left for collection behind the building. Opening the door she found herself face-to-face with the disembodied head of a man, which was floating in mid-air before her. Letting out an almighty scream, she raced back inside where landlady, Sarah Kennedy, calmed her down with a stiff brandy. Having regained her composure, the girl agreed that it might be best if she went upstairs for a rest. But no sooner had she got to the first floor landing, than she began screaming again. Her colleagues rushed to assist and found her looking aghast at a picture of Oliver Goldsmith that was hanging on the wall. 'That's him,' she cried, 'that's the face I saw.'

YE OLDE MITRE TAVERN
1 ELY COURT, EC1
London's Most Hidden Pub

Tucked away down a narrow alleyway that runs between Hatton Garden and Ely Place, Ye Olde Mitre Tavern is a true gem of bygone London. It dates back to 1546, and was built for the servants of the Bishop of Ely whose London palace then stood nearby. Indeed, the stone bishop's mitre that adorns one of the pub's outside walls once reputedly stood over the main gate of Ely Palace. Encased in glass by the door of the front bar are the remnants of an ancient cherry tree around which Elizabeth I is said to have danced the May Dance with one of her 'favourites' Sir Christopher Hatton, to whom she awarded Ely Palace, having evicted the then bishop.

From time to time, phan-tom footsteps have been heard ascending the steep, narrow staircase and entering the upstairs bar. When staff go to investigate they invariably discover that the room is empty, and there is no sign of anybody who could have been responsible for the footfall. Bar staff sitting in the back bar late at night have also heard some-one walking down the passage to the side of the pub and have been surprised by the outside door suddenly opening wide, although nobody is standing there when it does so!

SADLER'S WELLS THEATRE
ROSEBERY AVENUE, EC1
The Fears of a Clown

The recent and costly rebuilding of Sadler's Wells Theatre, belies the fact that it is one of London's oldest theatre sites, founded in 1683 by Thomas Sadler. In April 1781, Joseph Grimaldi (see also page 15) made his stage debut at the theatre when he was just three years old. He went on to enjoy a successful theatrical career, during which he almost single-handedly laid the foundations for the modern pan-tomime tradition. Grimaldi's macabre last request that his head should be severed from his body prior to burial was, apparently carried out and this might account for the chilling apparition that was frequently seen at the theatre prior to its rebuilding. His disembodied head, recognizable by its white-panned face and glassy eyes, was seen several times, floating behind the occupants in one of the old boxes. Intriguingly, the people occupying the box never had any idea that they had been honoured by an appearance until it was mentioned to them after the play! As yet there have been no reports of similar hauntings in the new theatre.

ABOVE: A portrait of the writer Oliver Goldsmith whose disembodied activities have shocked several bar staff at Ye Olde Cock Tavern.

OPPOSITE: The incredibly narrow Ye Olde Cock Tavern is still frequented by 18th-century patron, writer Oliver Goldsmith who is buried outside its back door.

> # 'THAT'S HIM,' SHE CRIED, 'THAT'S THE FACE I SAW.'
>
> THE BARMAID WHO SAW OLIVER GOLDSMITH'S GHOST

THE CITY & THE EAST END

THIS AREA OF LONDON is steeped in history and ghosts: from the spectral cries that echo over Smithfield Market to the shadowy monk who keeps a lone vigil inside London's oldest parish church, St Bartholomew the Great. We also stray into the gas-lit streets of the Victorian metropolis to ponder the infamous murders of Jack the Ripper. Pride of place belongs to the Tower of London which holds the dubious distinction of being the most haunted building in the whole of England!

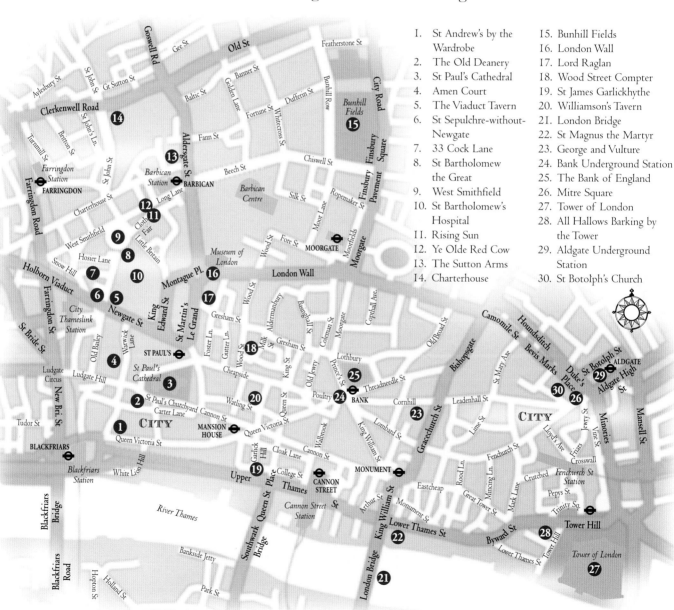

1. St Andrew's by the Wardrobe
2. The Old Deanery
3. St Paul's Cathedral
4. Amen Court
5. The Viaduct Tavern
6. St Sepulchre-without-Newgate
7. 33 Cock Lane
8. St Bartholomew the Great
9. West Smithfield
10. St Bartholomew's Hospital
11. Rising Sun
12. Ye Olde Red Cow
13. The Sutton Arms
14. Charterhouse
15. Bunhill Fields
16. London Wall
17. Lord Raglan
18. Wood Street Compter
19. St James Garlickhythe
20. Williamson's Tavern
21. London Bridge
22. St Magnus the Martyr
23. George and Vulture
24. Bank Underground Station
25. The Bank of England
26. Mitre Square
27. Tower of London
28. All Hallows Barking by the Tower
29. Aldgate Underground Station
30. St Botolph's Church

in Worcester in the 15th century, and it was an established piece of Avenbury folklore that, whenever a vicar of the church died, this particular bell would always ring of its own accord to mourn his passing. Barely a year after its arrival in London, local residents were woken in the early hours of one morning by the knell of a solitary bell, sounding from the tower of the church. When local police arrived to investigate they found the building was locked and a cursory search revealed no sign of a forced entry. The night was still, with not even the faintest breeze blowing, and yet many people had heard the bell tolling, though none could explain how – or why – it could have happened. The next morning word arrived that the vicar at Avenbury had died shortly before the mysterious chime was heard.

THE OLD DEANERY
DEAN'S COURT, EC4
The Ghost that Bemused the Dean

The Old Deanery was built in 1670 by Sir Christopher Wren (1591–1658) and was formerly the residence of the Dean of St Paul's Cathedral. There is a long held tradition that the building is haunted, although Martin Sullivan, Dean of St Paul's until his retirement in 1977, was ever willing to pour scorn upon the assertion. The strange groans and creaks that were often heard by members of his family and staff, he attributed to the antiquity of the building. The bumps and clanks that often shattered the quiet of the night hours he dismissed as 'nothing more than the central heating getting on a bit'. He did, however, confess to being slightly bemused by a toilet-roll holder that would go 'decidedly wonky' whenever anyone else looked at it, but which had always righted itself by the time he arrived to repair it. But then he added: 'Since I can't conceive of a haunted toilet-roll holder, I can only put it down to my skill at do-it-yourself.'

ST ANDREW'S BY THE WARDROBE
QUEEN VICTORIA STREET, EC4
Ask Not For Whom the Bell Tolls

The unusual name of this redbrick church, which was built by Sir Christopher Wren in 1695, refers to its former proximity to the King's Wardrobe, a suite of neighbouring buildings where robes of state and cloth for the royal household were stored. The buildings were destroyed during the Great Fire of London (1666), after which the wardrobe was moved to Westminster.

In 1933, three bells from the parish church at Avenbury, Herefordshire, were re-hung in the belfry of St Andrew's by the Wardrobe. One of them, known as Gabriel, had been cast

St Paul's Cathedral

St Paul's Churchyard, EC4

Whistler's Secret Doorway

Entering the magnificent interior of St Paul's Cathedral via the north-west door, you pass the Kitchener Chapel on the left. Its walls are adorned with an assortment of Battle Colours and a white marble effigy of Lord Kitchener (1850–1916), Secretary of War from 1914, reclines on its floor. Kitchener's death, on 3rd June, 1916, was treated as a national calamity. If, as you stand gazing upon his memorial, a sudden chill passes over you, take note, for this is often the first hint that the cathedral's ghostly resident, 'Whistler', is about to put in an appearance. Next, you will hear the low, barely audible sound of mournful whistling. Gazing into the chapel you may spy a wizened, old clergyman dressed in old-fashioned robes with flowing locks of grey hair. His doleful, though tuneless, whistling will grow steadily louder as he glides across the chapel and melts slowly away into the wall to the right of the gates. Everyone who has seen him attests to the fact that he always follows the same route and vanishes into the same section of the wall.

Intriguingly, during the renovation work following the 1914–18 War, when it was decided that the chapel – then known as the All Souls' Chapel – should be re-dedicated to Lord Kitchener, workmen uncovered a hidden door behind the exact section of wall where the ghost always disappears. It opened onto a narrow, winding staircase that led up to a secret room within the inner fabric of the main body of the cathedral. Nobody had known of its existence, or purpose, with, of course, the exception of the ghost, whoever he may have been in his lifetime.

Amen Court

Warwick Lane, EC4

The Realm of the Black Dog

Amen Court is a delightful, hidden enclave of 17th- to 19th-century houses, where the Dean and Chapter of St Paul's Cathedral live. Famous past residents have included wit and

ABOVE: Amen Court is haunted by the shuffling figure of a shapeless, black form known as the 'Black Dog of Newgate', which is said to date from the 13th century.

author Sydney Smith (1771–1845) who lived at number one between 1831 and 1834; and R. H. Barnham, author of the evocative and eerie *Ingoldsby Legends*, who occupied the same address from 1839 to 1845. At the rear of the court a large and ominous dark wall looms. Behind it once stood the fearsome bulk of Newgate Prison, which was demolished in 1902. However, there remains a tiny passage, which was known as 'Deadman's Walk'. The passage took its name from the fact that prisoners were led along it to their executions, and were buried beneath it afterwards.

Although many ghostly tales have evolved around this sinister old wall, the most chilling is that of the 'Black Dog of Newgate'. This shapeless, black form slithers along the top of the wall, slides sloppily down into the courtyard and then melts away. Its manifestations are always accompanied by a nauseous smell, and are often accompanied by the sound of dragging footsteps. Its origins are said to date back to the reign of Henry III (1207–72), when a fearsome famine struck London and the poor felons incarcerated within Newgate, faced with the prospect of starvation, turned to cannibalism as a means of survival. One day a scholar was imprisoned there on charges of sorcery. His portly figure proved too much of a temptation for the emaciated inmates and, within a few days, they killed and devoured him, pronouncing him to be 'good meate'.

However, the prisoners soon had cause to regret their actions, for a hideous black dog, with eyes of fire and jowls that dripped with blood, appeared in the dead of night and proceeded to exact a terrifying revenge. Some hapless prisoners were torn limb from limb by the ferocious beast, striking terror into the very souls of the other inmates as their anguished screams echoed through the gaol. Others simply died of fright when they heard the beast's ghostly panting and its heavy paws padding towards them across the cold, stone floors. Those who survived the first nights of the dog's lust for blood and vengeance became so terrified that they killed their guards and escaped. But no matter how far they travelled, the beast hunted them down one by one. Only when the murder of its master – the dead sorcerer – had been fully avenged, did the dog return to the prison's fetid dungeons, where it became a hideous harbinger of death, appearing on the eve of executions or on the night before a felon breathed his last. When Newgate was demolished in 1902, it was hoped that the black dog would become a thing of the past. But it was not to be. For people who happened to glance at the dark wall when walking in Amen Court at night, have occasionally reported seeing its seething black shape, shuffling across the wall, and have watched as it slithers into the courtyard where it disappears before their very eyes, leaving the smell of death in its ghostly wake.

Another ghost associated with the courtyard is that of Amelia Dyer, the 'Reading Baby Farmer'. Paid to look after unwanted babies, this evil woman drowned her charges in the Thames and other rivers, whilst continuing to draw a substantial income for their upkeep. Brought to justice, Amelia was sentenced to death and, on the 10th June, 1896, she took her final stroll along 'Deadman's Walk'. As she did

ABOVE: Child murderer Amelia Dyer, the 'Reading Baby Farmer' who haunted Newgate Prison.

so, she passed a young warder named Mr Scott. Stopping abruptly, she turned towards him slowly and fixed him with her evil gaze. Her dark eyes looked into his, her face cracked into a toothless smile and, in a low, rasping voice, she sneered, 'I'll meet you again some day, sir.' Moments later, she was dead, dangling at the end of the hangman's noose.

The years passed, Scott progressed in his chosen career, and memories of Amelia Dyer and her prophecy were soon forgotten. Then, just before the prison was to close, he found himself alone one night in the warders' room, his back to the grille that looked out onto Deadman's Walk. Suddenly, a cold shiver ran down his spine and he had the distinct impression that someone was watching him. Then he heard it, that low, sneering, rasp as the unmistakable voice of Amelia Dyer echoed from the passage: 'Meet you again, meet you again… ' Turning, he saw her evil, grinning face, framed by the grille. Stirred to action he rushed at her, but she promptly vanished. Throwing open the door, the passage was silent and empty. Had he imagined it? Possibly. Yet he could never account for the woman's handkerchief, which at that very moment, fluttered to the flagstones and lay still by his feet…

THE VIADUCT TAVERN
126 NEWGATE STREET, EC1
Down in the Cellar

The Viaduct Tavern stands opposite the Central Criminal Courts, better known the world over as the Old Bailey after the road in which they stand. The pub dates from 1875, and is the last example of a late Victorian gin palace left in the City of London. It is also prone to suffer from bouts of poltergeist activity.

The word 'poltergeist' is derived from two German terms: Poltern meaning 'to knock' and Geist meaning 'spirit'. The restless spirit that haunts The Viaduct Tavern has a propensity to haunt the pub's cellars and several members of staff have experienced its unwelcome attentions. One Saturday morning in 1996, a manager was tidying the cellar, when the door suddenly slammed shut and the lights went out. Feeling his way to the door, he discovered that, no matter how hard he pushed, it just would not open. Fortunately, his wife heard his cries for help and came downstairs to investigate. She found that the doors, which would not open from the inside, were unlocked and easily pushed open from the outside.

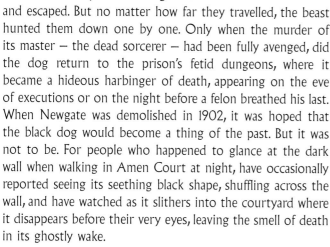

'I'LL MEET YOU AGAIN SOME DAY, SIR.' SHE SNEERED.

THE LAST WORDS OF AMELIA DYER, THE READING BABY FARMER

ABOVE: Despite claims to the contrary The Viaduct Tavern dates from 1875 and is haunted by a mischievous sprite called 'Fred'.

In May 1999, two electricians working in one of the pub's upstairs rooms, also attracted the ghost's unwelcome attentions. The pair had rolled the carpet up and were taking up the floor-boards, when one of them felt a hand tap him on the shoulder. Thinking it was his workmate he turned round, but found that he was on the other side of the room. Believing that he had imagined it he went back to work, only to feel another tap on his shoulder. Standing up, he went over to his friend to ask if he was playing a prank, but the man denied any involvement. As he was about to return to his chores, both men watched as the heavy carpet, which lay rolled up by the window, was lifted into the air and dropped heavily onto the floor.

ABOVE: 33 Cock Lane may now be long demolished but its ghost 'Scratching Fanny' can still be guaranteed to raise a smile!

St Sepulchre-without-Newgate
Holborn Viaduct, EC1
Don't Be Alarmed It's Just the Ghost

Originally dedicated to St Edmund, the Church of the Holy Sepulchre was founded in 1137. Like its namesake in Jerusalem, the church stood just outside the north-west gates of the city, and it was the favoured venue for the knights of the Crusades to set out from on their journeys to the Holy Land. For that reason it acquired its present name.

The church was rebuilt in 1450 and, although it was damaged by the Great Fire of London (1666), it wasn't destroyed, and thus the edifice that greets today's visitor is a veritable cornucopia of differing architectural styles.

During the Blitz in World War II, the nearby City Temple was destroyed, and its congregation was invited to make use of the Church of St Sepulchre, as it was by then better known.

As the vicar handed over the keys to the temple's minister, Dr Weatherhead, he commented casually that, if he were alone in the church at night and happened to see a tall, pale clergyman 'don't be alarmed; it's just a ghost'. The vicar went on to explain '... he's quite often there, and when I speak to him he never answers.'

Following the morning service a few Sundays later, Dr Weatherhead and his wife invited a female friend to dine with them. Over lunch, the woman, who had been told nothing of the haunting, informed the minister that on the occasions when she had watched him take communion at the church, she had noticed a 'tall, pale-faced clergyman, with you in the Sanctuary. At first I thought he was assisting you and then one morning I saw you walk right through him, and I knew he was a ghost.'

33 Cock Lane, EC1
Scratching Fanny

Cock Lane is now a relatively uninteresting thoroughfare whose chief glory is the cherubic fat boy that is perched high up on its north-eastern side, and which marks the spot where the Great Fire of London burnt itself out in 1666. Number 33 was demolished long ago, which is a great pity, for in the late 18th century one of London's most infamous hauntings occurred at what was then the home of William Parsons.

One morning in 1760, Parsons offered lodgings to a widower called William Kent. Kent gratefully accepted and moved in to the house with his sister-in-law, Miss Fanny, with whom he had become romantically involved. Not long after the two lovers had taken up residence, Parsons borrowed a considerable sum of money from Kent, but showed a marked reluctance to repay it. Relations were strained between the two men, when Kent was suddenly called away on business. Rather than sleep alone while her lover was away, Miss Fanny took Parsons's 11-year-old daughter, Elizabeth, into bed with her at night. In the early hours of the morning, they were woken by a mysterious scratching noise sounding from behind the wainscoting. Fanny convinced herself that it was the spirit of her dead sister, warning her of her own imminent demise. When Kent returned he found his mistress on the verge of a nervous breakdown and he deemed it best that they move out of the lodgings. However, no sooner had they found a new home, than Fanny died of smallpox, and was buried in a vault at St John's Church, Clerkenwell.

When Kent began to press Parsons for repayment of the outstanding loan, his former landlord reacted by claiming that

RIGHT: A ghostly monk walks the 'Holy Gloom' of St Bartholomew the Great, London's oldest parish church.

the scratching noises had resumed in his house. Furthermore, he insisted that the spirit of Miss Fanny was behind this latest outbreak, and that she had informed him that William Kent had actually murdered her. When news spread that a vengeful ghost was making its presence known at 33 Cock Lane, Londoners flocked to make its acquaintance. They heard the revenant of Miss Fanny – using a sequence of banging, scratching and knocking noises – accuse William Kent of poisoning her with arsenic. The ghostly activity appeared to centre on 11-year-old Elizabeth Parsons, and her father was only too happy to decipher the messages. He did a roaring trade by charging an admission fee to those who wanted to hear the ghost.

Then a local clergyman threw a holy spanner into the works by announcing that, since the spirit was apparently accusing Kent of a serious crime, an investigation into the veracity of the allegations should be carried out by a group of eminent men. The ghost proved more than willing to oblige and informed him, through Parsons, that if he spent a night by Miss Fanny's resting place in St John's Church, then she would answer any questions by knocking on the lid of her coffin. And so it was that the vicar, accompanied by a group of fearless companions that included the great Dr Samuel Johnson, traipsed down into the church vault at 1 a.m. one morning. When nothing had occurred by dawn, Johnson declared the ghost a fraud. However, a secret watch had been kept on Elizabeth, who was observed hiding a small wooden board beneath her stays, and the trick was exposed. Parsons spent two years in the King's Bench Prison. Elizabeth was exonerated of any crime as it was deemed that she had been an unwitting accomplice and William Kent's name was cleared. London settled back into the Age of Reason, and the ghost was consigned to the pages of history as 'Scratching Fanny of Cock Lane'!

ST BARTHOLOMEW THE GREAT
WEST SMITHFIELD, EC1
Footsteps in the Night

The Priory Church of St Bartholomew the Great is the oldest parish church in London. It possesses a dark and mysterious interior, the ancient walls of which drip with atmosphere. It has been used as a location for films as diverse as *Robin Hood Prince of Thieves* and *Four Weddings and a Funeral*. Its ambience has been described as the 'holy gloom' and it comes as

ABOVE: Smithfield market, Europe's largest market, stands on the Smoothfield where executions were once carried out.

little surprise to learn that the building is haunted. Even its beginnings are tinged with the supernatural. The church was founded in 1123 by Rahere, a man who, according to legend, was once a jester at the court of King Henry I (1068–1135).

In November 1120, Henry's son and heir drowned when the White Ship was lost in a winter storm off Calais. The court was plunged into despondency, and Rahere opted to become a monk and set off on a pilgrimage to Rome. Whilst there, he fell dangerously ill with malaria and vowed on his death bed that if he were cured and allowed to return to his own country, he would 'erect a hospital for the restoration of poor men.' Miraculously, Rahere's prayer was answered, and he duly set off for England. On his journey he had a terrible dream in which he was seized by a fearful winged creature and taken up onto a high ledge where he was set down, teetering on the brink of a yawning chasm. Just as he was about to fall, the radiant figure of St Bartholomew appeared at his side, and told Rahere that he had come to save him. In return, said the saint: 'in my

name thou shalt found a church… in London, at Smedfeld (Smithfield).' Thus the church was founded and Rahere was buried within it when he died in 1145.

His tomb now stands to the left of the altar, its reverse side clearly showing the results of a hasty repair carried out in the 19th century when the parish officials decided to report upon the state of the founder's body. It was well preserved, and even Rahere's clothes and sandals are said to have been intact. A few days after the tomb was sealed, one of the church officers fell ill and confessed that, when the tomb had been open, he had stolen one of the sandals. He gave it back and recovered, but it was never returned to the foot of its rightful owner, and since that day Rahere has haunted the church as a shadowy, hooded figure that appears from the gloom, brushes past astonished witnesses, and fades slowly into thin air.

On other occasions his appearances have been more active. In the mid-20th century the Reverend W. F. G. Sandwich was showing two ladies around the church when he sighted a monk standing in the pulpit, giving a very animated sermon to an unseen congregation – although no sound could be

Engraved for Fox's Book of Martyrs.

The Martyrdom of H. Adlington, L. Parnam, H. Wye, W. Hallywell, T. Bowyer, G. Searles, E. Hurst, L. Cawch, R. Jackson, J. Derifall, J. Routh, Eliz. Pepper, and Agnes George, at Stratford, Bow.
Published as the Act directs, for H. Trapp Pater-noster Row.

G. Terry Sculp.

Pater noster Row.

heard. The two ladies appeared to be oblivious to the appari-tion, but just to be sure, the Reverend Sandwich directed their attention to the pulpit observing: 'I don't think that pulpit is worthy of the church, do you?' The ladies merely agreed with him, obviously quite unaware of the ghostly monk.

In May 1999, John Caster, the verger of the church who lived in the house next door, was woken early one morning by a tele-phone call from the security company, informing him that the alarms were going off inside the church. Entering the building he turned on the lights and conducted a brief search. The church was empty. Switching the lights off, he was about to leave, when he clearly heard the measured tread of slapping foot-steps, walking down the central aisle. He called out, 'who's there?' whereupon the footsteps stopped for a moment. Then they con-tinued along the aisle. Convinced there was an intruder, he locked the doors and called the police. They arrived within min-utes, but could find no sign of anyone inside the building. Furthermore, no windows or doors were open. The next morn-ing the security company sent an engineer to check and reset the motion-triggered alarms. Both he and John were astonished to discover that only the central beam — the one that passes Rahere's tomb — had been broken. The beams by the doors, and the side and top aisles had not been breached, which meant that whatever, or whoever, was responsible, had somehow managed to simply 'appear' at the centre of the church. It was then that John remembered that the footsteps had sounded like sandals, slap-ping over the stone floor of the old church.

ABOVE: During the reign of 'Bloody Mary' close on 200 Protestants were burnt alive for their faith.

WEST SMITHFIELD, EC1
Death by Fire and its Ghostly Effects

The 'Smoothfield', as Smithfield was originally known, was for many years one of London's many places of execution. In August 1305, Sir William Wallace — Braveheart — was put to death here, and a grey granite plaque on the wall of St Bartholomew's hospital still commemorates the Scotsman's heroic exploits. In the reign of Queen Mary Tudor (1553–58) over two hundred Protestants were put to death in England, and many of them were burnt at Smithfield. 'Bloody Mary', as she was known, was emphatic that green wood should not be used, as its smoke was likely to suffocate the victims before they suffered the full agony of the flames. We can only guess at the terrible suffering endured by those who perished here, as Mary strove to undo the work of her father Henry VIII and her brother Edward VI, and bring Catholicism back to the people of England, using fire and the sword. For some of her victims, the torment appears to have proved eternal. Those who work in the area in the early hours of some mornings, have often been disturbed by anguished and agonized screams that rend the air, and by the sickly smell of burning flesh that is carried upon the night breeze.

ST BARTHOLOMEW'S HOSPITAL
WEST SMITHFIELD, EC1
The Haunt of the Grey Lady and the Coffin Lift

St Bartholomew's, or Bart's as it is known to those who study and work there, has the distinction of being the oldest hospital in London to stand on its original site. Its origins stretch back to 1123, when it was founded as part of the monastery of St Bartholomew by Rahere (see page 48), a court jester, turned man of God.

In the depths of the hospital there is an elevator, which generations of doctors and nurses have come to know as the 'coffin lift'. In the silent hours of early mornings, the lift has been known to take bemused passengers down to the basement, irrespective of which floor they have requested. Once there, its lights go out and the lift does not move. After a few moments of madly pushing the lift's buttons, staff are able to pull open the gates and walk back up to the ground floor. Here they find the lift waiting, its gates open and its lights on. Should they then choose to walk up to the level they requested,

they suffer the unnerving experience of having the elevator follow them up the lift shaft, around which the staircase twists. Tradition maintains that the ghost responsible for the malfunction is a nurse who was once murdered in the lift by a deranged patient.

The spirits of former nurses haunt other parts of the hospital. Grace Ward is the spectral domain of the 'Grey Lady', a nurse in old-fashioned uniform who, in life, is said to have administered a fatal overdose to a patient and to have killed herself in remorse. Now, if ever modern nurses are about to make a similar mistake, they are said to feel a light tap on their shoulders and, looking up, they see the Grey Lady shaking her head in warning. A similarly attired lady has been seen on Bedford Fenwick Ward, although she appears to administer comfort. Nurses have long grown used to patients asking them to thank the old-fashioned nurse for bringing them a cup of tea shortly before they die.

RISING SUN
38 CLOTH FAIR, EC1
Where Body Snatchers Once Lurked

The Rising Sun is a cosy and traditional 18th-century hostelry that lay derelict and empty for much of the 20th century until Tadcaster brewer Samuel Smith purchased and refurbished the building in 1984. Its proximity to St Bartholomew's Hospital has led to a local tradition that in the early 19th century, a gang of body snatchers used the pub as a meeting place and a hunting ground for cadavers with which to supply the research needs of doctors. Whether there is any truth in the rumour that this dastardly band would replenish their merchandise by drugging and murdering patrons of the Rising Sun is debatable. But what is certain, is that some historical act of infamy has left a psychic stain upon the pub's ethereal plain and managers and staff have encountered several ghosts over the years. Two Brazilian barmaids who worked and lived here in 1989 were often woken in the early hours, by a 'presence' that sat on the end of their beds, and that would occasionally tug the bed-clothes off them slowly. Several bar men who have been cleaning up in the downstairs bar late at night, have been disturbed by the distinct sounds of footsteps running across the

LEFT: Cloth Fair is one of the last enclaves of Elizabethan London to have survived into the modern age.

floor of the upstairs bar. However, on investigation they discovered that the room was always empty. Finally, in 1990, the landlady of the time was enjoying a shower in the staff bathroom one summer's afternoon when she thought she heard the bathroom door open and close. The next moment, the shower curtain was pulled slowly aside and an ice-cold hand ran down her back. She turned around quickly, but found the that she was alone.

YE OLDE RED COW
71 LONG LANE, EC1
Dick O'Shea Keeps a Ghostly Watch

Ye Olde Red Cow is a snug little pub that stands opposite Europe's largest market, Smithfield Meat Market. The butchers and meatpackers work throughout the night, and so many of the pubs in this area have special licences that allow them to open between the hours of 6.30 a.m. and 9 a.m. Ye Olde Red Cow is one of these market pubs, and for many years in the late 20th century, it was run by Dick O'Shea, a characterful Irishman, who numbered amongst his clientele the actors Peter Ustinov and Bernard Miles. They, along with many others, were attracted here by Dick's legendary hot whiskey toddies. Ever the benign host, once the pub opened at 6.30 a.m. Dick sat in a favoured rocking chair on the upper balcony, rocking back and forth, as he kept a genial and watchful eye on the comings and goings below. He died in 1981, but his spirit apparently found it difficult to adjust. For almost a year after his demise, regulars in the bar below caught frequent glimpses of his unmistakable form, sitting in his rocking chair, a warm smile upon his face, as genial and watchful a host in death as ever he had been in life.

ABOVE: In the early 19th century few bodies were safe from the nefarious activities of the body snatchers or 'Resurrectionists'. However, modern medicine owes them an eternal debt of gratitude.

THE SUTTON ARMS
6 CARTHUSIAN STREET, EC1
Charley's Ghostly Antics

Behind the enchanting, bow-windowed frontage of the Sutton Arms, is a snug and cosy interior that is haunted by a red-haired old gentleman in old-fashioned dress who, as they have never been formerly introduced, the landlord has come to know as 'Charley'. The ghost has been seen sitting nonchalantly in a corner of the pub, and on one occasion, he appeared suddenly between two girls who were enjoying a lunchtime drink. Having given them a nasty fright, he grinned and then promptly disappeared. One night in October 1997, a friend of the landlord, who was staying in one of the pub's upstairs rooms, was looking in the mirror and combing her hair, when a cold shiver suddenly passed over her. The next moment she saw the reflection of a smiling, red-haired man standing behind her. She spun around quickly to remonstrate with the intruder, but was astonished to find nobody there.

ABOVE: Charterhouse courtyard is visited by the ghost of a monk and the 16th-century Duke of Norfolk.

OPPOSITE: John Bunyan is just one of the non-conformists whose mortal remains lie in Bunhill (Bone Hill) Fields. In 2001, gardeners reported some alarming occurrences.

CHARTERHOUSE
CHARTERHOUSE SQUARE, EC1
A Haunted Gem of Hidden London

The ancient wall of weathered stone that encircles the Charterhouse — London's only surviving Tudor town house — helps keep the contemporary world firmly at bay. Beyond the massive oak gates of the gatehouse, visitors find themselves in a veritable time capsule, the origins of which stretch back to 1371 when Norman nobleman Sir Walter de Manny endowed a monastery for the strict order of the Carthusian monks. Here the holy brethren offered prayers for the souls of those who died in the Black Death of 1348, many of whom still lie buried in the great square outside the gates. The monastery flourished until the Reformation, when its monks refused to accept Henry as head of the Church in England. Their prior, John Houghton, was hanged, drawn and quartered, and one of his arms was even nailed onto the monastery gates in an attempt to persuade the surviving monks of Henry's cause. But, inspired by their leader's bravery, and ghostly nocturnal visits from long dead members of their order urging them to

remain true to their faith, the friars remained firm and refused to curtail to the king's demands. One dark, wintry night, as they prayed in the dimly lit chapel, there came a flash of heavenly flame, which caused every candle to flare up with a celestial brilliance. Encouraged in their battle with the State, the monks remained steadfast, even though 16 more of their number were executed before the monastery was finally dissolved.

Charterhouse was then granted to Lord North, who turned it into a splendid private residence. He entertained Elizabeth I here on two occasions, but his hospitality was so lavish that he crippled himself financially and had to retire to the country. Thomas Howard, 4th Duke of Norfolk, then bought the house. His plans to marry Mary, Queen of Scots resulted in his execution in 1572, and the house had several more owners before being purchased in 1611 by the immensely wealthy Sir Thomas Sutton (1532–1611). He converted the building into a hospital for aged men and a school for the sons of the poor. In time the establishment became a distinguished public school, moving to new premises in Godalming, Surrey in 1867. Today some 20 or so elderly men live amid the ancient courts and forgotten cloisters of this wonderful old mansion.

When the surrounding streets fall silent at night, a shadowy monk is said to drift aimlessly about the cobblestone courtyards, parts of which survive from the days of the monastery. He shares his weary vigils with the headless spectre of the Duke of Norfolk, which comes striding down the main staircase where he was arrested, with his head tucked neatly under his arm.

BUNHILL FIELDS
CITY ROAD, EC1
When the Dead Walked Again

The name of this ancient city burial ground, which is crammed with an eclectic mix of tombs and gravestones, is probably derived from Bone Hill. Since there is no proof that the ground here was ever consecrated, it was a favoured burial place for non-conformists, who were able to bury their dead without the use of the Common Prayer Book. John Bunyan (d. 1688), Daniel Defoe (d. 1731) and William Blake (d. 1827) are just a few of those whose graves are shaded by soaring plane trees. The spiked gate at the graveyards north-east

'THINGS HAVE GONE A BIT HAYWIRE IN THE LAST TEN MONTHS... LOADS OF WEIRD STUFF HAS STARTED HAPPENING.'

A GARDENER'S DESCRIPTION OF SUPERNATURAL EVENTS AT THE BUNHILL FIELDS GRAVEYARD

a safe haven from whatever supernatural forces were loose in the fields, began to suffer the attentions of the ghostly residents. Bill Underwood told how he had unlocked the door one morning, and found 'all our posters and notices had mysteriously been taken down and arranged neatly on the floor in exactly the same order.' Strange handprints had also appeared on the table, which certainly did not belong to any of the staff. Asked if he had any idea who or what was responsible for the activity, Bill could only shrug his shoulders and express bemusement.

LONDON WALL, EC2
A Ghostly Arm

In April 1907, a letter appeared in the *City Press* concerning the old section of the London Wall that now cowers beneath the gleaming white modernity of the Museum of London. A reader told how he had been passing this relic one Sunday night, when he noticed a hand and arm 'stretched out from the railings to bar my passage.' He was so alarmed by this that he jumped into the road and, for a moment, turned his back to the railings. On summoning up the courage to look round, he saw a man in dark clothes, walking back to the wall. When he reached it he 'seemed to walk right into it.' The bemused witness recalled how he had heard no sound of footsteps, and told how he had returned the next morning to examine the spot but could find nothing that threw any light on the mystery of what, or who, it was that he had encountered.

ABOVE: Bunhill Fields where, in 2001, a head gardener commented on an outbreak of supernatural activity with the words: 'Things have gone a bit haywire.'

corner was put up specially to deter the nefarious activities of the body snatchers. Although no burials have taken place here since 1854, the Corporation of London still maintains the ground for public usage and employs several gardeners to ensure that this vast necropolis remains in pristine condition.

In June 2001, several of the gardeners complained of experiencing supernatural phenomena. 'Things have gone a bit haywire in the last ten months,' one of them told the *Highbury and Islington Gazette*, '… loads of weird stuff has started happening.' Steam was seen rising from graves; several gardeners spoke of encountering a cloaked woman who suddenly disappeared without trace; whilst floods of water would suddenly appear from nowhere, even on dry days. Meanwhile, the gardeners' hut, which had long been considered

LORD RAGLAN
61 ST MARTINS-LE-GRAND (ALDERSGATE STREET), EC1
The Ghostly Roman

This lively 19th-century hostelry stands close to part of the old city wall, which was originally constructed by the Romans to enclose Londinium. The cellars are built onto much older foundations and it is there that several of the staff in the early 1990s were frequently surprised by a ghostly Roman sentry whose 'indistinct' figure would 'quiver' in one of the corners, seemingly oblivious to their presence. After a few moments the soldier would become even hazier and then simply fade into nothing.

WOOD STREET COMPTER
MITRE COURT, EC2
A Slice of Bygone London

Tucked away in Mitre Court, at the heart of the City of London, a dark canopy, covering a dingy flight of uneven steps, leads the intrepid wayfarer down into a dark, dingy cellar. This was once, so local tradition maintains, the common section of a debtors' prison known as the Wood Street Compter. The prison was demolished in 1816, but the eerie cellar has survived. However, its condition is so poor that – thanks to the compensation culture that now blights so much of our everyday life – public access is forbidden until such time as we can learn to take responsibility for our own wellbeing once more.

Until recently, the Four Vintners Off Licence, whose shop was in Mitre Court, leased the site, and they would often use the cellar for wine tasting evenings. One night in 1986, an assistant was tidying up after one such session, when she was pushed from behind with such violent force that it caused her to drop the three bottles of wine that she was holding. Even today, with the off licence gone and the gates padlocked to prevent access, some people passing the cellar late at night claim to sense a 'presence' watching them from the gloomy darkness below. Some have even heard, a low, murmuring whisper that appears to emanate from behind the locked door at the bottom of the steps.

ST JAMES GARLICKHYTHE
GARLICK HILL, EC4
Jimmy Garlick, the Ghostly Mummy

In 1855, workmen clearing out a vault in this particularly exquisite Wren church, uncovered a casket that contained the mummified corpse of a man. Parishioners, nicknamed him 'Jimmy Garlick', and having encased him in glass, placed him in the church's entrance porch, along with a salutary note that read:

ABOVE: The mummified remains of 'Jimmy Garlick' lie in a room in the Tower of St James Garlickhythe. However, his skeletal spectre has been known to wander downstairs from time to time!

Stop Stranger As You Pass By.
As You Are Now So once Was I.
As I Am Now So Shall You Be.
So Pray Prepare To Follow Me.

There was a time when impish choirboys would remove Jimmy on Sunday mornings, sitting him in one of the pews with a ruff around his neck, all of which the corpse appears to have accepted with good humour. Then, in the Second World War, a bomb dropped through the roof of the porch and, although it didn't explode, it landed uncomfortably close to the cabinet, shattering its glass. This appears to have stirred

ABOVE: Once the guardian of Old London Bridge, St Magnus the Martyr is one of the city's haunted churches.

Jimmy's revenant to indignation, and his ghost has wandered the church ever since. Not long after the incident, a fire-watcher spotted a dark figure walking along the aisle during an air raid. He shouted at the figure to take cover, whereupon it simply vanished. In the 1970s an American tourist visited the church with her two sons, the elder of whom went off to explore alone. Climbing the stairs to the balcony, he came face to face with a skeletal figure, its hands crossed over its chest. The dumbfounded boy was rooted to the spot as the phantom stared at him, its eyes bulging from its bony sockets. Finally the boy was able to cry out to his mother, whereupon the mysterious apparition melted away before his eyes.

Jimmy's mortal remains are now kept away from public gaze in an upper room of the church tower. He is now thought to have been 16-year-old Seagrave Chamberlain, who died from a fever on 17th December, 1765, and whose wall monument can be seen at the west end of the north aisle.

WILLIAMSON'S TAVERN
1 GROVELAND COURT, BOW LANE, EC4
The Dead Centre of the City

Williamson's Tavern is a delightful, well-hidden hostelry that has more the feel of a gentlemen's club than of a city centre pub. It stands at the exact centre of the City of London, reputedly on the site that was once occupied by the mansion of Sir John Oldcastle, the model for Shakespeare's Falstaff. Once the official residence of successive Lord Mayors of London, it was purchased in 1739 by one Robert Williamson, who turned it into a hotel. William Hollis, a surveyor who rebuilt it in the 1930s, quickly found that his dabbling had apparently disturbed a former resident. According to contemporary accounts, 'queer noises' were heard about the premises on Saturday nights. Furthermore, a ghostly figure was often seen gliding from the opposite side of Groveland Court and melting into the brickwork of the pub. Although the apparition never materialized inside the buildings, its perambulations were often accompanied by an outbreak of poltergeist activity, during which tankards and ashtrays would be hurled to the floor by an unseen hand. The disturbances finally proved too much for Mr Hollis to bear and so, according to a report in the *City Post*, he decided to 'leave the ghost to its own devices... and the estate is now on the market.'

LONDON BRIDGE, EC4
A Tragedy from Long Ago

Old London Bridge used to stand a little further down river from the current span. The churchyard of St Magnus the Martyr provided pedestrian access to it, and there is a long held tradition that the reach of the Thames that flows past the church is haunted by ghostly cries.

In 1290, Edward I (1239–1307) ordered the expulsion of all Jews from England. One group hired a ship to take them abroad, and it was arranged with the captain that they would set sail from just below London Bridge. However, their vessel was caught on an ebb tide and became beached upon the river sands. The captain suggested that they leave the ship to wait for the turn of the tide on a nearby sandbank. As the tide began to rise, the captain and crew raced back to the ship, leaving the hapless passengers to drown in the rising waters. The exact spot where the callous event occurred is uncertain, but there is a strong Jewish tradition that it was beneath London Bridge. The ghostly screams of the victims are said to echo down the centuries, and, according to one Anglo-Jewish writer, the spot where it happened 'is under the influence of ceaseless rage; and however calm and serene the river is elsewhere, the place is furiously boisterous.'

ABOVE: Old London Bridge was the site of an horrific tragedy and the screams of the victims can still be heard today.

ST MAGNUS THE MARTYR
LOWER THAMES STREET, EC3
The Kneeling Cleric

The Church of St Magnus the Martyr has a peaceful air about it. To the right of the altar a plaque on the wall commemorates Miles Coverdale (1488–1568), who was rector of the church from 1563 to 1565. He is best remembered as the man who, as Bishop of Exeter, instigated the first English translation of the Bible. However, many who stand over the spot where his earthly remains lie interred claim to have been overcome by a sudden and intense feeling of grief and desolation. The feeling has sometimes been accompanied by the appearance, moments later, of a dark haired priest in a black cassock, seen stooping over the vault where Coverdale lies entombed. This has led to speculation that the ghost is that of Miles Coverdale himself.

An electrician who once spent several days working in the church complained of a priest who kept watching him, and who had the annoying habit of being there one moment but gone the next. A verger who had locked the church one Sunday night and was tidying up, suddenly noticed a dark haired priest, standing a few feet away from him. He was about to ask how the man had managed to enter a locked building, when the figure dropped to its knees and began searching for something on the floor. Stepping forward to offer assistance, the verger was surprised when the priest looked up at him, grinned and promptly disappeared!

GEORGE AND VULTURE
ST MICHAEL'S COURT, CORNHILL, EC3
The Victorian Lady

The George and Vulture was established in 1600 and was the place where Sir Francis Dashwood (1708–81) founded his notoriously nefarious Hell Fire Club. Charles Dickens was a regular visitor in the 19th century and used it as Mr Pickwick's London base in *The Pickwick Papers*. Its walls are adorned with images of both Dickens and his characters, and its upstairs rooms are occasionally visited by a Victorian lady in a grey dress who floats silently about before astonished witnesses, until, after a few moments of restless roaming, she melts slowly into thin air.

BANK UNDERGROUND STATION, EC1
The Stench from Beyond the Grave

Bank Underground sits at the historic hub of the City of London, and is surrounded by such venerable institutions as the Bank of England, the Royal Exchange and the Mansion House, which is the home of the Lord Mayor throughout his year in office. In addition to its being an extremely busy miasma steep down into the tunnel and drift towards Bank Station, afflicting the nostrils and the sensibilities of the London Underground maintenance workers?

THE BANK OF ENGLAND
THREADNEEDLE STREET, EC2
The Bank Nun

On 2nd November, 1811, Philip Whitehead, 'a man of genteel appearance' who had been employed in the cashier's office at the Bank of England, was brought to the dock of the Old Bailey charged with forgery. Found guilty, he was sentenced to death and was duly hanged in early 1812. However, the news of his crime and execution was kept from his devoted sister, Sarah Whitehead, who was removed by Philip's friends to a house in Wine Office Court, off Fleet Street. One day, Sarah turned up at the Bank of England to enquire of her brother's whereabouts, and an unthinking clerk promptly blurted out the story of Philip's crime and ignominious death. The shock of the discovery turned the poor woman's mind and thereafter she took to turning up at the bank every day and asking after her brother in the belief that he still worked there. She became known as the 'Bank Nun' on account of her peculiar attire, which consisted of a long black dress and a black crepe veil worn over her face and head. The city merchants took pity on her and never let her pass 'without extending their assistance', whilst the directors and clerks of the Bank of England saw to it that she was frequently provided with 'sums of money in compliment of her misfortune'.

ABOVE: The Bank of England. Should a lady in black ask if you have seen her brother as you pass the Bank of England, do not worry, it is only the ghost of Sarah Whitehead.

station, it is also haunted. It is the maintenance workers, whose unenviable task it is to attempt to keep the Central Line running, that have most often experienced supernatural activity here in the early hours of some mornings. They report having been overcome by a foul stench – 'like the smell of an open grave' is how one employee described it. In its wake there comes a dreadful feeling of foreboding and melancholy. It may be connected with the fact that the next station along the line, Liverpool Street, is believed to have been built on the site of a 17th-century plague pit. Is it possible that something from all the decomposing bodies that were buried together has impregnated the soil hereabouts? And when conditions are right, does some form of

However, Sarah became convinced that the bank's governors were keeping an immense fortune from her and this led to her hurling insults at them during business hours. On one occasion Baron Rothschild was going about his business at the Stock Exchange when she suddenly appeared and called him a 'villain and a robber' telling him that he had defrauded her of her fortune and demanding the £2,000 he owed her. He responded by taking half a crown from his waistcoat pocket, handing it to her and telling her as he did so: 'There, then, take that and don't bother me now; I'll give you the other half tomorrow.' Accepting the money, she thanked him and went away.

ABOVE: A police drawing of Mitre Square in September 1888 when Catherine Eddowes, Jack the Ripper's fourth victim, was murdered there.

By 1818 the Bank governors had grown tired of her daily disturbances and so gave her a sum of money on condition she agreed never to return to the bank again. In life she kept that contract, but in death her wraith has broken it many times. More than one late-night wanderer, wending their weary way home along Threadneedle Street has been surprised by her ghostly figure appearing before them and, with downcast eyes, enquiring sadly, though politely: 'Have you seen my brother?'

MITRE SQUARE, EC3
A Poignant Wraith

Today, Mitre Square is surrounded on three sides by modern office blocks and bordered on its south side by the Sir John Cass Foundation School. Nothing remains of the original Victorian square, save its cobblestones, across which people hurry on their way to and from work, many not even realizing that they are walking over the spot where one of London's most infamous crimes occurred. For it was in the south-west corner of Mitre Square that the horribly mutilated body of Catherine Eddowes was discovered at 1.45 a.m. on 30th September, 1888 – the fourth victim of the murderer history remembers simply as 'Jack the Ripper'. Local tradition maintains that, on the anniversary of the

killing, people have occasionally glimpsed Catherine's spectral figure lying upon the spot where her life came to such a tragic and gruesome end.

TOWER OF LONDON
TOWER HILL, EC3
England's Most Haunted Building

Grim, grey and awe-inspiring, the Tower of London has dominated the London landscape and the pages of its history since its construction by William the Conqueror in 1078. Today, it is perhaps the most haunted building in England.

The Wakefield Tower is haunted by that most tragic of English monarchs, the pious King Henry VI (1421–71), whose weak and ineffectual reign ended here with his murder as he knelt at prayer 'in the hour before midnight' on 21st May, 1471. Tradition asserts that the knife with which he was 'stikk'd full of deadly holes' was wielded by the Duke of Gloucester, later the infamous Richard III (1452–85). On the anniversary of his murder, Henry's mournful wraith is said to appear as the clock ticks

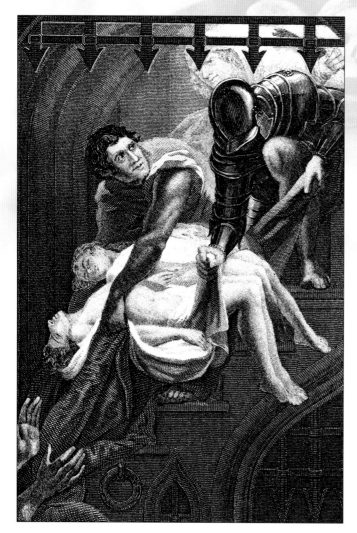

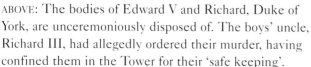
ABOVE: The bodies of Edward V and Richard, Duke of York, are unceremoniously disposed of. The boys' uncle, Richard III, had allegedly ordered their murder, having confined them in the Tower for their 'safe keeping'.

RIGHT: The Tower of London, once the living quarters of monarchs, became the site of royal executions, the victims of which continue to haunt the site of their hapless demise.

towards midnight, pacing fitfully around the interior of the Wakefield Tower until, upon the last stroke of midnight, he fades slowly into the stone and rests peacefully for another year.

The massive White Tower is the oldest and most forbidding of all the Tower of London's buildings and its winding stone corridors are the eerie haunt of a 'White Lady' who once stood at a window waving to a group of children in the building opposite. It may well be her cheap perfume that has caused many a guard to retch upon inhaling its pungent aroma and which impregnates the air around the entrance to St John's Chapel. In the gallery where Henry VIII's impressive and exaggerated suit of armour is exhibited, several guards have spoken of a terrible crushing sensation that suddenly descends upon them as they enter the room, but which lifts the moment they stagger, shaking, from it. A guard patrolling through the chamber one stormy night got the sudden and unnerving sensation that someone had thrown a heavy cloak over him. As he struggled to free himself, the garment was seized from behind and pulled tight around his throat by his phantom attacker. Managing to break free from its sinister grasp, he rushed back to the guardroom where the marks upon his neck bore vivid testimony to his brush with the unseen assailant.

A memorial on Tower Green remembers all those unfortunate souls who have been executed here over the centuries. Anne Boleyn (1507–36) and Lady Jane Grey (1537–54) are both said to return to the vicinity, whilst the ghost of Margaret Pole, Countess of Salisbury, returns to the site in

a dramatic and alarming fashion. At the age of 72 she became an unwitting and undeserving target for Henry VIII's petty vengeance. Her son, Cardinal Pole had vilified the King's claim as head of the Church in England. But he was safely ensconced in France and so Henry had his mother brought to the block on 27th May, 1541. When told by the executioner to kneel, the spirited old lady refused. 'So should traitors do and I am none,' she sneered. The executioner raised his axe, took a swing at her and then chased the screaming countess around the scaffold where he literally hacked her to death. The shameful spectacle has been repeated several times on the anniversary of her death, as her screaming phantom continues to be chased throughout eternity by a ghostly executioner.

The Bloody Tower, the very name of which conjures up all manner of gruesome images, is home to the most poignant shades that drift through this dreadful fortress. When Edward IV died suddenly in April 1483, his 12-year-old son was destined to succeed him as Edward V. However, before the boy's coronation could take place, both he and his younger brother, Richard were declared illegitimate by Parliament and their uncle, the Duke of Gloucester ascended the throne as Richard III. The boys, meanwhile, had been sent to the Tower of London, ostensibly in preparation for Edward's Coronation, and were often seen playing happily around the grounds. But then, in about June 1483, they mysteriously vanished, and were never seen alive again. It was always assumed, that they had been murdered on Richard's instructions and their bodies buried somewhere within the grounds of the Tower. When two skeletons were uncovered beneath a staircase of the White Tower in 1674, they were presumed to be the remains of the two little princes and afforded royal burial in Westminster Abbey. The whimpering wraiths of the two children, dressed in white nightgowns, and clutching each other in terror have frequently been seen in the dimly lit rooms of their imprisonment. Witnesses are moved to pity and long to reach out and console the pathetic spectres. But, should they do so, the trembling revenants back slowly against the wall and fade into the fabric.

Returning to the White Tower, and the fearless Custody Guards who wander its interior in the dead of night, there was the eerie occasion when Mr Arthur Crick decided to rest as he made his rounds. Sitting on a ledge, he slipped off his right shoe and was in the process of massaging his foot, when a voice behind him whispered: 'There's only you and I here.' This elicited from Arthur the very earthly response: 'Just let me get this bloody shoe on and there'll only be you!'

ABOVE: One of the Tower of London's most gruesome executions was that of the elderly Margaret Pole who, having refused to go willingly, was hacked to death by her executioner.

gazing down upon the smouldering remnants of the city below, declared it 'the saddest sight of desolation'.

At about 6 p.m., a few days before Christmas 1920, a choirmaster and two choirboys had gone into the church to rehearse. They had been singing for around 20 minutes when they noticed an old lady standing a few feet away from them. So real did she appear that one of the boys walked over and placed a chair for her to sit on, the woman nodded her thanks and sat down. She was dressed, so the choirmaster later recalled, in old-fashioned clothing. Her hair was grey and her face had sallow features. But what struck him most about her was the intense look in her eyes. 'They seemed to burn with a strange radiance… and were fixed on my face as if eagerly searching for something, or as if fascinated by our music.' Their strange visitor mystified the choirmaster. He had certainly locked the door when they had entered, so how could she have got inside? Also, how had she managed to approach their rehearsal room without any sound? He had heard no footsteps on the stone floor and, furthermore, the heavy, creaking double doors that led from the main body of the church had been silent since he and the choristers had passed through them. Then, just as the practice concluded, the mysterious visitor vanished suddenly without trace. No sooner had she done so, than a strange scratching noise sounded from a corner of the room, 'as if a cat was in the building and was trying to get out'. Suddenly one of the boys cried out in alarm 'There it is sir! I saw a cat rush out of the room and go down towards the south aisle!' They searched the church but could find no trace whatsoever of either the woman or the cat. Furthermore, when they went to leave the building, the door was still locked.

Five years later, the choirmaster was standing in the church one Sunday morning when an old man approached him and told him that he believed he knew the identity of the old woman. He explained how, around 60 years previously, he had been a choirboy at the church and that a somewhat

ALL HALLOWS BARKING BY THE TOWER
BYWARD STREET, EC3
The Lady in Black

The mark of history is certainly upon the ancient church of All Hallows by the Tower. Through its doors have stepped such illustrious personalities as Bishop Lancelot Andrewes (1555–1626) and William Penn (1644–1718), who were christened here in 1555 and 1644 respectively. The infamous Judge Jeffries was married at the church in 1667, as was John Quincy Adams (1767–1848) – later sixth President of the United States – in 1797. After the Great Fire of London (1666), Samuel Pepys climbed to the top of its tower and, eccentric lady organist had led the choir in those days. She was 'passionately fond of… cats,' the old man told the choirmaster, and continued, '… cats used to follow her about, even in the streets… she used to give me pocket money for feeding them regularly. She was "quite gone" on carols, and used to take us boys through the city lanes… singing them as well as in church.'

Is it possible that the former choirmistress's love of carols continued beyond the grave, and that it was her ghost that had appeared in the church on that December night? Certainly the description given by the old gentleman of her style of dress corresponded exactly with clothing worn by the apparition in the rehearsal room. Furthermore, reports of her appearances continued throughout the 1920s and early 1930s. Sadly — or happily, depending on how you view these things — she seems to have found lasting rest in recent years, for many decades have passed without any reports of the ghostly old lady at All Hallows Church.

ALDGATE UNDERGROUND STATION
ALDGATE HIGH STREET, EC3
A Real Live Wire

Aldgate Station is situated at a convergence of rail lines to the east of the city. In the 1950s an electrician was carrying out essential maintenance on the rail tracks, when a station manager happened to glance towards him and was surprised to see a grey-haired old lady, stroking the man's head. Moments later, a mistake in the control room sent 22,000 volts surging down the track, and although the electrician was thrown backwards and knocked unconscious, he survived the surge of current through his body, and suffered no lasting ill effects. Ever afterwards he remained grateful to the mysterious, grey-haired 'guardian angel' whom he was convinced had saved his life.

Aldgate Station certainly has a decidedly spooky air about it and over the years other ghostly activity has occurred here. Most persistent is the ghostly sound of footsteps echoing across the sleepers late at night. These are often accompanied by cheerful whistling, as though some contented rail man from days gone by is carrying out a ghostly track inspection.

ST BOTOLPH'S CHURCH
BISHOPSGATE, EC2
The Ghost in the Photograph

In 1982, photographer Chris Brackley took a picture inside this historic old church. The only people present were himself and his wife. When the photograph was developed he was

ABOVE: Did a ghostly figure make an appearance in Chris Brackley's photograph of St Botolph's Church taken in 1982?

astonished to note that a woman in old-fashioned garb was standing on the balcony to the right of the altar. The negative was subjected to considerable expert analysis, which revealed that that there was no double exposure to the film and it was also proved that none of Chris's equipment was faulty. The only explanation for the mysterious figure was that someone must have actually been standing on the balcony when the picture was taken.

A few years later Chris was contacted by a builder who had been employed on restoration work in St Botolph's crypt. He explained that he had inadvertently disturbed a pile of old coffins when knocking down a wall. One had come open to reveal a reasonably well-preserved body, the face of which bore an uncanny resemblance to the figure that had made an uninvited appearance in Chris's photograph.

WESTMINSTER TO KNIGHTSBRIDGE

WESTMINSTER, THE ROYAL CITY, is home to a diverse collection of ghosts. From the poignant ghostly soldier in Westminster Abbey to the headless spectre that occasionally rises from the tranquil waters of the lake in St James's Park. The chapter also includes a look at the ghosts that haunt the residence of Britain's Prime Minister, and looks at the two phantoms that roam the rooms and corridors of Buckingham Palace. Heading west we discuss the haunting at the Royal Albert Hall before moving on to take a look at England's most haunted bed!

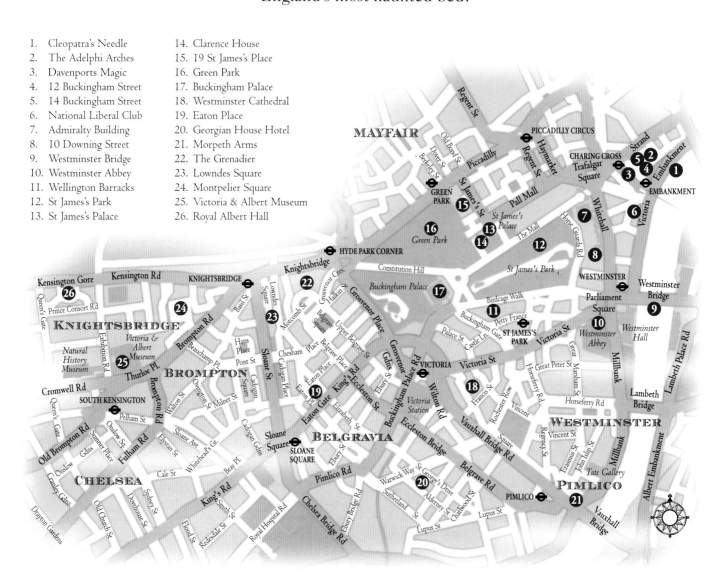

CLEOPATRA'S NEEDLE
VICTORIA EMBANKMENT, WC2
A Mysterious Encounter on a Foggy Night

Originally erected outside the Temple of the Sun at Heliopolis by Pharaoh Thotmes III in 1450 BC, this mysterious obelisk was moved to Alexandria in 14 BC, hence its association with the legendary Egyptian Queen. It was brought to London in 1878 and has stood proudly on the banks of the River Thames ever since.

It seems to hold a particular attraction to those of a despondent nature, for it is acknowledged that more suicides occur on the reach of the Thames that flows past it than on

PREVIOUS PAGE AND BELOW: More suicides take place around Cleopatra's Needle than on any other stretch of the River Thames. Could it have anything to do with the low moan that passers-by have reported in the late evening?

any other part of the river. People passing the column at night have occasionally been startled by the sound of a low moaning that they hear emanating from within the dark granite. Others have spoken of their alarm when a shadowy, naked figure sprints across the riverside terrace and throws itself over the wall towards the river. But no splash is ever heard, and those who go to investigate never see anyone floundering in the water, nor is any body discovered.

But one of the most mysterious events to have occurred in the vicinity of this most enigmatic of monuments took place in the 1940s, when a hysterical young woman suddenly approached a policeman crossing over nearby Waterloo Bridge one foggy night. She told him that someone was about to jump into the Thames, and begged him to follow her in order to prevent the tragedy. The constable followed her through the dense fog and arrived at Cleopatra's Needle just in time to prevent a young woman from throwing herself into the murky waters of the racing river. As he pulled the suicide back from the brink, he was astonished to find himself face to face with the young woman who had just alerted him on Waterloo Bridge. Turning to where she had been standing a few seconds earlier, he could find no trace of her whatsoever.

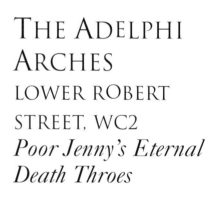

THE ADELPHI ARCHES
LOWER ROBERT STREET, WC2
Poor Jenny's Eternal Death Throes

The delightfully gloomy Lower Robert Street descends into one of the only surviving 18th-century arches, built to support the buildings of the Adelphi — a prestigious housing development by the Adams brothers. By the 19th century, according to one account, 'the most abandoned characters... often passed the night [here], nestling upon foul straw; and many a street thief escaped from his pursuers in these dismal haunts...' In *David Copperfield* Charles Dickens has the protagonist recall: 'I was fond of wandering about the Adelphi, because it was a mysterious place with those dark arches... ' The ambience of this subterranean vault is still sufficient to elicit cold shivers, and it comes as little surprise to find that this place of silent shadow is haunted. One of the desperate characters to whom the arches were home was 'Poor Jenny', a Victorian prostitute who was strangled by one of her clients on the grim bundle of filthy rags that she used as her bed. Today Jenny's terrifying, pain-racked screams, followed by a rhythmic drumming, as her feet repeat her death tattoo upon the stones, occasionally echo through the dingy vault, shattering the stillness and chilling the marrow of those who happen to be in the vicinity.

DAVENPORTS MAGIC
5–7 CHARING CROSS UNDERGROUND ARCADE, WC2
As if from Nowhere

Davenports is the oldest family magic business in the world, and from the moment the dull thud of a loud bell announces your arrival, you get the sensation of having entered a truly hidden gem of secret London. A veritable cornucopia of all things magical and mysterious confronts you. Ferocious-looking arm choppers, complete with plastic severed limbs, glimmer behind glass display cases. There are ESP and Tarot cards, and all

ABOVE: Visitors to Davenports Magic Emporium may encounter more than a rabbit appearing from a hat!

manner of disappearing, appearing, perturbing and bemusing apparatus for initiation into the secretive world of magicians and psychics. The shop is haunted by what staff maintain is a 'male presence'. Several of the assistants, who enthusiastically demonstrate their dexterous skills at sleight of hand before wide-eyed visitors, have caught glimpses of someone walking to the side of the counter towards the stock room. However, whenever they go to investigate, there is never anyone there. At other times, items have been moved around in the storeroom, which can prove a little annoying for staff trying to despatch an urgent order. This latter activity though is easily dealt with by the ruse of simply asking the ghost to desist and return whatever object it is that has disappeared.

12 BUCKINGHAM STREET, WC2
Mr Pepys is Still at Home

This handsome house, now home to Regent Language School, was the home of the celebrated diarist Samuel Pepys (1633–1703) between 1679 and 1688. Several people have reported witnessing his ghost here and describe it as 'a greyish figure, with a smiling, kindly face'. He has been seen strolling briskly down the main staircase, or even looking down onto passers-by in the street below.

In the early 1950s Gwyneth Bickford, who worked in the offices that occupied the property at that time, was running down the staircase at about 7 p.m one evening, when she suddenly noticed a man dressed in the costume of the 17th century, standing against the wall. 'He was not a bit transparent,' she later recalled. 'He was smiling with his lips and with his eyes as if he was tremendously pleased to see me… His outline was slightly blurred and his whole appearance grey. We just stood there looking at each other for what I suppose was a couple of seconds, and then he was gone.'

14 BUCKINGHAM STREET, WC2
The Buxom Phantom

Number 14 Buckingham Street was once the home and studio of William Etty (1787–1849), an artist who was famed for his sensuous Victorian nudes. The 'happy, buxom, girl ghost' that haunts the property, and which appears in the hallway from time to time, is thought to be the spectre of one of his models.

NATIONAL LIBERAL CLUB
WHITEHALL PLACE, SW1
Knock Knock

With its dark, eye-catching turrets the National Liberal Club is a local landmark that frequently draws the attention of those who pass it on the Victoria Embankment. During the 1890s the rooms occupied by the club's secretary and his family were subjected to an alarming bout of poltergeist activity that included mysterious knocking noises, which seemed to emanate from deep within the walls. The family duly carried out an intensive investigation and, by a process of careful elimination, discovered that the phenomenon only seemed to occur when a certain German servant girl was present. Although convinced that the girl was in no way consciously responsible for the activity, the secretary sacked the unfortunate servant and, thereafter, the activity ceased.

ADMIRALTY BUILDING
WHITEHALL, SW1
Martha Ray the Politician's Friend

The dark brick Admiralty Building was built in the 1720s by Thomas Ripley, and was later extended to become Admiralty House, home of the First Lord of the Admiralty. In the latter half of the 18th century the office was held by the 4th Earl of Sandwich (1717–92), who brought his mistress, Martha Ray to live here with him. Having borne him several children, Martha embarked upon an affair with a penniless army lieutenant called James Hackman. Although the two fell deeply in love, Hackman lacked the means to support Martha and, when she refused to leave the earl, her heartbroken lover left the army and became an equally impecunious clergyman.

Then one night in April 1779, Hackman spotted Miss Ray passing along Whitehall en route to a performance of *Love in a Village* at the Covent Garden Theatre. Insane with jealousy, he rushed home and fetched a pair of pistols with which, he later claimed, he intended to shoot himself before the eyes of his mistress. Instead, he shot Martha dead as she emerged from the theatre. The crime was witnessed by virtually the entire audience of the play, so there was little doubt as to his guilt. However, the passion of the crime together the romance of the story, thrilled polite society. The Earl of Sandwich, in a gesture of moving forgiveness, provided Hackman with financial assistance during his imprisonment and trial. Found guilty, Hackman was sentenced to death and subsequently executed.

Martha Ray has haunted Admiralty House ever since her murder and was seen in the early 20th century by both Winston Churchill and Harold Macmillan. In June 1969, several newspapers reported that Denis Healey – who as Secretary for Defence was then occupying quarters in the building – and his family were being visited by her restless wraith. Healey was reported to have seen her ghost on several occasions and even went as far as to tell reporters that his children, far from being frightened by her, were actually very fond of 'the lady' and had come to accept her as part of the family!

10 DOWNING STREET, SW1
The Prime Minister's Haunted Abode

In 1732 George II gave 10 Downing Street to his Prime Minister, First Lord of the Treasury, Sir Robert Walpole (1676–1745). Since then, the house has been considerably extended and altered and has been both home and office to successive British Prime Ministers. Several ghosts are known to haunt the building. One is a man in Regency-style clothing

ABOVE: Murdered actress Martha Ray has made many a ghostly return to the Admiralty building on Whitehall. Even Winston Churchill reported seeing her.

OPPOSITE: Visitors to 12 Buckingham Street may well encounter the happy spirit of the diarist Samuel Pepys.

who makes fleeting appearances both inside and outside the house. Nobody knows who he is, although there is a suggestion that he may be a former Prime Minister. During extensive alterations made to the building during the late 1950s and

ABOVE: The smell of tobacco wafting through the basement of 10 Downing Street has been attributed to the ghost of Winston Churchill smoking cigars.

early 1960s workmen are said to have encountered the ghost several times. On one occasion his shimmering shade was even seen in the garden, where it moved towards the wall that backs onto Horse Guards Parade and disappeared.

A lady in a long dress and wearing a magnificent set of pearls haunts the Pillared Drawing Room, which is used today for official functions and the signing of international agreements. Several messengers as well as people working in the neighbouring offices have reported both seeing and hearing her phantom. Meanwhile, policemen on guard duty have heard ghostly footsteps plodding their way around the building, although they can never find anyone in the vicinity when they go to investigate.

The basement of 10 Downing Street is the spectral realm of a little girl who has been known to hold the hands of those walking along its corridors. It is also where several employees have reported smelling the overpoweringly strong odour of cigar smoke wafting around the rooms. Some wonder if the ghost of Winston Churchill (1874–1965) might still be hanging around and enjoying the odd cigar from time to time.

Finally there is the smartly dressed spectre in a top hat who has been seen striding determinedly across the entrance lobby, and has been known to make a decidedly unconventional exit — straight through the closed front door!

WESTMINSTER BRIDGE, SW1
The Ghostly Leap of Jack the Ripper

If you stand on Westminster Bridge on 31st December and look eastwards as midnight approaches, you may well be rewarded with a sighting of the ghost of one of London's most enigmatic criminals. For there is a local tradition that, as the first chimes of Big Ben usher in the New Year, a shadowy figure will suddenly materialize on the parapet, and leap headlong into the murky waters of the River Thames below. Legend maintains that this is the hour when Jack the Ripper killed himself by plunging into the river from this spot in 1888, and that every year since, his wraith has been condemned to repeat his descent into infamy over and over again.

Should a festive visit be out of the question a spectral barge has been known to drift towards the bridge on misty autumn mornings, pass beneath it and vanish before reaching the other side.

WESTMINSTER ABBEY, SW1
The Ghostly Monk and the Unknown Soldier

In the 6th century the area of Westminster was an inhospitable island that rose from the marshy banks of the River Thames at the point where Tyburn Stream joined it. It was the location chosen by Serbert, the newly converted king of the East Saxons, on which to build a church dedicated to St Peter. The church was to be consecrated by Mellitus, the first Bishop of London. Legend tells how, on the night before the consecration, a fisherman rowing along the south bank of the Thames was stopped by a cloaked stranger who asked to be taken across the river. As the vessel reached the opposite shore, the new church was suddenly illuminated in a celestial

brilliance and singing angels filled the blazing night sky. The stranger then revealed himself to be St Peter, and having anointed the church's walls with holy water, he proceeded to dedicate his church.

For almost 500 years afterwards, a Benedictine abbey flourished on the site until Edward the Confessor (c. 1001–68) rebuilt it. A few days after the abbey's re-consecration in January 1066, Edward died, and Harold was crowned king. But in October of the same year, Harold was defeated by William of Normandy at the Battle of Hastings, and on Christmas Day 1066, William the Conqueror (1027–87) was crowned king in the abbey, beginning the tradition of coronations taking place there.

Over the centuries that followed Westminster Abbey was considerably expanded and altered and, in the process, the level of the floor was progressively lowered. This may explain why the ghostly monk who is known to haunt the building is seen floating a little way off the ground. He is known as 'Father Benedictus' and is most often seen bobbing around the cloisters in the early evening. His spectral figure appears quite solid, and he has been known to hold conversations with

witnesses, many of whom do not realize that he is anything other than flesh and blood. In 1900, he kept a group of visitors entertained for a good 25 minutes as he drifted around the cloisters and then backed slowly towards a wall where he melted into the fabric. In 1932, two American visitors even held a long conversation with him, later commenting that they found him to be extremely polite.

Westminster Abbey's Tomb of the Unknown Warrior is a poignant memorial to the soldiers who died in World War I. On 11th November, 1920, the body of an unidentified soldier was given a state funeral. He was buried in soil that had been brought from the battlefields of France, and placed beneath a marble stone that had been quarried in Belgium. From time to time when the crowds have left and the abbey settles into quiet stillness, a ghostly soldier materializes alongside the tomb, and stands for a few minutes with his head bowed, before slowly dissolving into thin air.

WELLINGTON BARRACKS
BIRDCAGE WALK, SW1
The Headless Lady Travels

At around 1.30 a.m., on 3rd January, 1804, George Jones of the Coldstream Guards was on sentry duty at the Recruit House (now the Wellington Barracks). Suddenly a headless woman began to emerge from the ground about two feet in front of him. He observed that the figure 'was dressed in a red stripe dress, with red spots between each stripe...' and that 'part of the dress... appeared to be enveloped in a cloud...' Moments later the apparition had vanished and 'in great trepidation' the startled sentry reported the incident to his commanding officer. Jones discovered that several other soldiers had reported similar encounters in the vicinity. Indeed, many of them, according to a later report in *The Times*, were 'taken ill immediately and sent to hospital... from the effects of fright...', so affected were they by the night-time gambols of this ghost. Since at least one of the soldiers reported that the ghost had drifted over to the lake in St James's Park before

BELOW: A headless woman has been known to rise from the still waters of the Lake in St James's Park.

disappearing, there is little doubt that the ghost is the same one that haunts the area around the lake.

The headless ghost's nocturnal manifestations are not just confined to the distant past. In 1972, a motorist driving along Birdcage Walk crashed into a lamp post as he swerved to avoid a woman in a red dress who had suddenly appeared before him. Amazingly, the history of the haunting was brought up at the subsequent court case and the motorist was acquitted of dangerous driving!

ST JAMES'S PARK, SW1
The Headless Lady of the Lake

St James's Park was originally laid out for James I (1566–1625) in 1603 and was re-landscaped for Charles II in 1660. It was Charles who introduced the exotic waterfowl whose descendents still inhabit the park today. The lake was re-modelled between 1826 and 1827 by the Regency architect John Nash (1752–1835), by which time it had already acquired the spectral resident that has chilled the blood of many a late night wanderer hereabouts. A headless woman has been seen rising from the rippling waters of the lake. She drifts slowly onto dry land, where she suddenly breaks into a frenzied run, her arms

flailing wildly about her. Petrified onlookers stand, rooted to the spot, as the macabre apparition rushes into the bushes and disappears.

In life, the phantom figure is thought to have been the wife of a sergeant of the Guards, whose husband murdered her, decapitated her and buried her head at a secret location before flinging her body into The Canal, as the lake was then called. Since that day, her headless cadaver has roamed St James's Park, a restless phantom condemned to search in vain for her missing head.

ST JAMES'S PALACE
ST JAMES'S STREET, SW1
The Sickly Smell of Ghostly Blood

Built by Henry VIII, St James's Palace remained one of the principle residences of the kings and queens of England for more than 300 years. Its most famous haunting, however, dates from the first half of the 19th century. In the early hours of 31st May, 1810, the brother to George IV and William IV, Ernest Augustus, Duke of Cumberland (1771–1851), was awoken from a deep sleep at around 2.30 a.m. by what he thought was a bat fluttering around his chamber. The next thing he knew, he was subjected to a ferocious attack, as a sharp bladed weapon began slashing at his padded nightcap and gown. The duke attempted to deflect the blows, but his hands and wrists were cut, and he screamed for help in desperation. A valet by the name of Cornelius Neale rushed to assist him, and found the duke's regimental sabre lying on the floor by the door, covered in blood.

A doctor was summoned, and, as his wounds were being treated, Cumberland asked for his other valet, Joseph Sellis, to be sent for. Two servants went to rouse him, but as they approached his room, they were startled by a strange gurgling sound from within. Opening the door, they found Sellis lying dead on his bed. His throat had been cut back to the spine and his head was almost severed from his body. A hastily convened inquest concluded that the dead valet had, for reasons

ABOVE: St James's Palace, official home of the monarch and haunted by the shade of a murder victim that leaves a sickly sweet smell in its wake.

unknown, attempted to murder his master, and had returned to his room to commit suicide in remorse.

Court gossip, however, had a different take on the matter, and talk of a cover-up was rife. Some said that Cumberland had actually murdered Sellis and pointed out that the valet's hands were found to be clean although there was bloodstained water in his wash-basin. Would the valet, the doubters wondered, have had the time or the inclination to wash his hands,

CLARENCE HOUSE
THE MALL, SW1
The Old Duke of Connaught

Built in 1825 for the Duke of Clarence, who later became William IV, Clarence House was for many years the London home of Her Majesty, Queen Elizabeth, the Queen Mother (1900–2002). Following her death, the house became the abode of her beloved grandson, Prince Charles. From 1900 until his death in 1942, Arthur, Duke of Connaught, the third son of Queen Victoria, lived at Clarence House and it is his ghost that is reputed to haunt it.

During World War II the palace was transformed into the offices for the Foreign Relations Department of the British Red Cross Society. One Saturday afternoon, a year or so after the Duke's death, a recently employed clerk named Sonia Marsh was working alone in the vast building. She became decidedly uneasy and was convinced that someone – or something – was watching her. Peering into the darkness beyond her desk, she saw a greyish, misty, triangular shape drifting towards her. Petrified, she leapt to her feet, grabbed her coat and rushed from the building. When she returned to work on the following Monday morning she told a colleague of her experience. 'Oh don't worry,' came the reassuring reply, 'It was probably the old Duke of Connaught we see him all the time!'

19 ST JAMES'S PLACE, SW1
When Death's Herald Came

St James's Place is a quiet enclave hidden away from the busy main thoroughfares of London's West End. Number 19 is a slightly dilapidated building that is painted a vivid shade of yellow, and seems to cower behind the larger surrounding properties. For much of the 19th century, two spinster sisters, Ann and Harriet Pearson, owned the house. The two sisters were deeply devoted to one another, and when Ann died in 1858 Harriet opted to live alone in the house they shared for so long.

In November 1864, Harriet was taken ill whilst visiting relations in Brighton. She was brought back to her house in London, and her two nieces, Mrs Coppinger and Miss Emma Pearson, and her nephew's wife Mrs John Pearson moved in to nurse her. On 23rd December a heavy snowstorm swept across the capital and a thick mist descended upon St James's Place. Mrs Coppinger and Miss Pearson retired to bed, leaving Mrs Pearson to look after their ailing aunt. They left the bedroom door open and the gaslight on the landing burning. At around 1 a.m. the women were suddenly woken by a movement in their room. Both saw their dead Aunt Ann drift past their door, apparently heading for the sick room. Then, Mrs Pearson came rushing into their room panting that she had seen the dead woman enter the room and cross to Harriet's bedside.

ABOVE: The delightfully set back St James's Place has changed little since the 19th century when a one off haunting here became the talk of London.

having apparently almost cut his head off? Several alternative scenarios were soon circulating as to what had really happened. One version maintained that Sellis had found the duke in bed with his wife and, in an ensuing struggle, had been killed to stop him exposing Cumberland's adultery. Another theory held that Cumberland had seduced Sellis's daughter who, finding herself with child, had killed herself. When Sellis confronted his employer, the Duke had silenced him forever to avert a scandal. In the mid-19th century, an even wilder theory had it that the Duke and his other valet, Neale, were involved in 'the grossest and most unnatural immorality', and that Sellis, having caught them in the act, was murdered on the Duke's orders.

Whatever the truth, there are occasions when the old palace has settled at night when the ghost of Sellis has been seen walking the corridors, a gaping wound across his throat, the sickly sweet smell of fresh blood trailing in his spectral wake.

Nervously the three women returned to Harriet's room, where they found her awake. She told them that her sister's ghost had just come to her in order to call her away. Moments later the old lady had slipped into a coma and, having lingered for most of that day, she died at around 6 o'clock in the evening.

GREEN PARK, W1
The Tree of Death

The land now occupied by Green Park is reputed to have been the burial ground for the nearby St James's Hospital for Leprous Women, the site of which was commandeered by Henry VIII (1490–1547) for the building of St James's Palace. It is this that is said to account for the park's lack of flowers. Park-keepers whisper in hushed tones about one particular tree that has a reputation so sinister that it is known as the 'Tree of Death'. No birds sing in its branches, dogs avoid it, courting couples never indulge their passion beneath it and a feeling of melancholic gloom is said to hang heavy around it. This may account for the high number of suicides that have been found hanging from the branches of the tree. Some people passing by it in the fading light of day have been startled by a throaty, gurgling chuckle, which emanates from deep within its trunk. Others have caught glimpses of a tall, shadowy figure standing beside the tree and pointing at them. However the figure vanishes the moment anyone brave or curious enough walks towards it.

BUCKINGHAM PALACE
THE MALL, SW1
A Ghostly Monk and a Suicidal Spectre

Built in 1703 for John Sheffield, the Duke of Buckingham (1648–1721), Buckingham House became a royal palace when it came into the ownership of George III, who began an extensive restoration that would continued through the reigns of George IV and William IV (1765–1837). Queen Victoria (1819–1901), however, was the first monarch to actually live in the palace, since when it has been the principal London home of all her successors. Tradition maintains that, long before the palace was built, a monk at the monastery that once occupied the site was involved in an indiscretion that resulted in his being starved to death in the punishment cell. Presumably his death occurred over the festive period as his ghost only returns to haunt Buckingham Palace on Christmas Day. He always appears on the terrace that overlooks the gardens to the rear of the building. Bound in heavy chains he clanks and moans his way backwards and forwards along the terrace for a few chilling moments, before fading slowly away.

ABOVE: Should the Royal family deign to spend Christmas at Buckingham Palace they might well make the acquaintance of its ghostly monk.

A more contemporary ghost of the royal residence is that of Major John Gwynne, who was a private secretary to King Edward VII (1841–1910). Following a scandalous divorce that left him ostracized by polite society, Gwynne retired to his first-floor office one night, took his revolver and shot himself dead. Since then, staff working in the vicinity have occasionally heard the sound of a gun firing from the room where the suicide occurred, but always find the room is empty whenever they go to investigate.

WESTMINSTER CATHEDRAL
FRANCIS STREET, SW1
The Dissolving Cleric

On every count Westminster Cathedral is an impressive foundation. Dedicated to the Blood of Our Lord Jesus Christ, it is a soaring red brick Gothic extravaganza, with a spectacular Byzantine interior ablaze with mosaic-work and ornamented was plummeting to the ocean bed, his wife was holding an 'at home' in their house in Eaton Place. Suddenly Sir George, resplendent in his full naval regalia, appeared before over a hundred guests, strolled across the room and vanished. Lady Tryon did not see him herself and was mystified when told by her guests that her husband had just walked through the room. She explained that he was far away at sea. Next day, however, word reached her of the tragedy and she realized that her guests must have seen her husband's ghost.

GEORGIAN HOUSE HOTEL
35–39 ST GEORGE'S DRIVE, SW1
Haunted Hospitality

The building that houses the Georgian House Hotel dates back to the mid-19th century and has a timeless ambience. The hotel is haunted by several ghosts, including that of an unknown man who has been seen in one of the basement staff rooms. Whether or not this is the same ghostly figure that has been seen in the kitchen and one of the top floor bedrooms is unknown. Suffice it to say he, or they, are harmless enough revenants that are more than content to appear for a few fleeting moments and then be gone about their business. The ghosts of two children have also been seen flitting about the upper floors of the building. On one occasion, a manageress even held a conversation with them and assured them that, as the Georgian House Hotel is a friendly and hospitable place they were more than welcome to visit. However, she asked only that they confine themselves to the upper floors because their presence on the lower levels might prove disturbing to their living peers. To date, the ghostly juveniles have honoured her wishes!

MORPETH ARMS
58 MILLBANK, PIMLICO SW1
It Lurks in the Cellar

This Grade II listed building occupies a pleasant enough location, affords riverside views, and stands close to the Tate Britain art gallery. It was built in 1845 by a pub specialist called Paul Dangerfield, and was intended to serve the wardens of the notorious Millbank Penitentiary, which, until its demolition in 1890, stood on the site now occupied by the Tate. Accounts differ as to exactly who haunts the pub, although they all agree that he was a prisoner at the nearby jail and that he died in the pub cellar. One version of the tale maintains that he was a convict who, rather than face the prospect of being transported to Australia, hanged himself from a basement beam. Another version holds that the ghostly convict was in fact attempting to escape from Millbank when he dropped dead in

ABOVE: Admiral Tryon's spirit was seen at his house in Eaton Place at the exact moment when his real self was plummeting to the bottom of the Mediterranean.

with over 100 different types of marble from quarries all over the world. Although the Catholic Church strenuously denies that the cathedral is haunted, reports have occasionally trickled out of ghostly figure, swathed in black robes, which has been seen in the vicinity of the High Altar. In July 1966, a sacristan on night duty saw and challenged the figure, only to watch it dissolve into nothingness before him!

EATON PLACE
BELGRAVIA, SW1
The Admiral's Doppelgänger

On 22nd June, 1893, Admiral, Sir George Tryon was on manoeuvres with the Mediterranean Fleet off the coast of Syria. Suddenly he gave orders for his ship the Victoria, and the nearby Camperdown to turn inwards and steam towards each other. It was obvious to all on board that disaster was imminent, but none of his subordinates dared overrule or question Tryon's extraordinary command. In consequence, the two ships collided and the Victoria sank, taking the Admiral and four hundred mariners to a watery grave. As the ship went down Sir George was heard to say: 'It is entirely my fault.'

At more or less the exact moment that Sir George Tryon

the pub's cellar. Whatever the cause of his death, and whichever of the two men he was, his spirit remains at the pub to annoy and bemuse staff by, among other things, snatching bottles from their hands and smashing them on the floor.

THE GRENADIER
18 WILTON ROW, BELGRAVIA, SW1
A-haunting We Will Go

Wilton Mews is a delightful hidden nook, that is tucked away from the rush of modern London, and has a decidedly country village air about it. Colourful cottages line the cobblestones, and nestling within its tranquil serenity is one of London's most enchanting pubs, The Grenadier. Reputedly, the pub's upper floors were once used as the officers' mess of a nearby barracks, whilst its cellar was pressed into service as a drinking and gambling lair for the common soldiers.

It is here that a young subaltern is said to have been caught cheating at cards. His comrades punished him with such a savage beating that he died from his injuries. Although the year in which this occurred is not known, the month when it happened is believed to have been September, as this is when the pub experiences an onslaught of supernatural activity. A solemn, silent spectre has been seen moving slowly across the low-ceilinged rooms. Objects either disappear or else are mysteriously moved overnight. Unseen hands rattle tables and chairs, and a strange, icy chill has been known to hang in the air, sometimes for days on end. Footsteps have been heard pacing anxiously around empty rooms, whilst every so often a low, sighing moan has been heard emanating from the depths of the cellar. On one occasion a Chief Superintendent from New Scotland Yard was enjoying a drink in the pub, when wisps of smoke began to waft around him. His curiosity aroused, he reached towards the apparent source of the smoke, and with a cry of pain, pulled his hand quickly back as an invisible cigarette burnt it.

LOWNDES SQUARE
KNIGHTSBRIDGE, SW1
The Face-pulling Phantom

Lowndes Square has always been considered a fashionable address, and at least one former resident has been known to

ABOVE: September is the month to visit The Grenadier in Wilton Row if you wish to sample its other spirits.

return and gaze upon the smart houses that surround it. There have been several reports of people wandering in the square and encountering a white-haired old lady sitting by the kerb in an old-fashioned bath chair, and pulling faces at anyone who happens to look at her. She is reputedly the ghost of an old woman who, in the early part of the 20th century, suffered a stroke and was brought to live with her daughter and her family in Lowndes Square. On sunny days, the daughter placed her mother in her bath chair, and wheeled her into the street so that she could watch the world go by. Because the stroke had deprived her of the power of speech, the old woman communicated by pulling faces, and when she wanted to be taken back inside she grimaced at passers-by until one of them rang the bell of her house, and she could be moved indoors.

MONTPELIER SQUARE
KNIGHTSBRIDGE, SW7
She Came Back to Save her Husband's Soul

Montpelier Square was laid out in the mid-19th century on land that had once belonged to a wealthy Huguenot family called the Moreaus. Originally it was not considered a particularly good address, and it wasn't until the 1890s that its star began to wax, and it became a sought after place to live.

In 1913 a vicar was leaving a nearby church when an agitated lady approached him and told him that a man living nearby was seriously ill and that, concerned for the state of his soul, he wished to consult with a man of God. The clergyman went with her to a waiting taxicab, and the two were driven to an imposing house in Montpelier Square. The vicar climbed out of the taxi, walked up to the door and knocked loudly. When the butler answered, he confirmed that the man whom the lady had named did indeed live at the house, but added that his master was in good health and certainly had no need of the priest's services. Mystified, the vicar looked round for an explanation, but there was no sign of either the woman or the taxicab. At that moment the owner of the house appeared at the door and invited the vicar inside. 'It is very strange,' said the man, 'that you have been sent on such an errand in such a mysterious way... though I am perfectly well, I have been troubled lately about the state of my soul, and I have been seriously contemplating calling upon you...'

The clergyman stayed for a few hours as the man unburdened his conscience, and it was agreed that his new acquaintance would come to church the next morning, and that they would continue their discussion after the service.

However, the man failed to appear at church the next morning, and having ended the service, the vicar came back to the house to see what the matter was. He was met by the butler, who told him that his master had dropped dead suddenly — just 10 minutes after the vicar had left him the previous evening. The vicar was led up to the room where the man's body lay. Here, on the table, he happened to notice a portrait of the lady who had fetched him to the house the previous evening. 'Who is this?' he asked. 'That sir,' replied the butler, 'is my master's wife, who died 15 years ago.'

> ## 'THAT SIR,' REPLIED THE BUTLER, 'IS MY MASTER'S WIFE, WHO DIED 15 YEARS AGO.'
>
> A BUTLER TELLS THE LOCAL VICAR HE WAS SUMMONED BY THE GHOST OF HIS LATE MASTER'S WIFE

VICTORIA AND ALBERT MUSEUM
CROMWELL ROAD, SOUTH KENSINGTON, SW7
The Great Bed of Ware

On display in the Victoria and Albert Museum, this impressive piece of furniture, which measures an incredible 11 feet 1 inch long by 10 feet 8½ inches wide, has the dubious distinction of being the most haunted bed in Britain. Although it actually dates from about 1590, legend has bestowed upon it an older and more illustrious pedigree. It was, so tradition claims, made especially for King Edward IV (1442–83) by carpenter Jonas Fosbrooke in 1463 and intended for the sole use of the monarch. When Edward's son, Edward V (1470–83), became one of the tragic 'Princes in the Tower', the bed was sold and passed through the bedrooms of a succession of inns at Ware in Hertfordshire. On one occasion in the 17th century, 12 married couples are reputed to have shared the bed during a festival when there was literally, no room at the inn! However, the delightfully stuffy spirit of Fosbrooke did not take kindly to riff raff enjoying the luxury of his creation. He disturbed the slumber of anyone who dared sleep in the bed by pinching and scratching them in a most malicious and unpleasant manner. Indeed, so well known were his spectral attacks that it was once customary for guests at the various inns to drink a toast to the bed and the ghost before retiring for the night.

ROYAL ALBERT HALL
KENSINGTON GORE, SW7
Father Willis and the Ladies of the Night

The Royal Albert Hall stands on the site of Gore House the former home of Marguerite, Countess of Blessingdon (1789–1849), whose extravagant lifestyle and subsequent bankruptcy led to her abandoning England for Paris, where she died in poverty. Alexis Soyer (1809–58) then transformed the house into a flamboyant restaurant, but this was forced to close within five months. The Royal Commissioners for the Great Exhibition purchased the property, demolished the house and built the Royal Albert Hall on the site in commemoration of Queen Victoria's husband Prince Albert.

Several ghosts are said to haunt the building. The first is that of Henry 'Father' Willis who designed the 150-ton organ, which had an impressive 9,000 pipes and was the

ABOVE: The Royal Albert hall, haunt of a ghostly organ builder and two Victorian 'ladies of the night'.

largest instrument of its kind when it was built. Dressed in Victorian clothing his ghost has been seen wandering around the hall at night. The building's other spectres are more controversial, and are based upon a local tradition that Gore House was temporarily used as a brothel prior to its demolition. Each November, two Victorian 'ladies of the night' are said to roam along the upper gallery level and can be seen walking into one of the toilets. Their arms are linked and they remain oblivious to any comment made by those who encounter them. Indeed, as one employee at the hall put it: 'It is as though they are walking in their time not ours'.

WEST LONDON

In this chapter we delve into the ghosts that haunt London's western suburbs. Kensington Palace and Holland House give up their spectral secrets before we head to Notting Hill and an encounter with what must surely be one of England's most bizarre hauntings: a phantom double-decker bus. Having taken in a churchyard where the ghost may well make its 50-year appearance in 2005, we head out to the glorious Chiswick House where the chance of a ghostly breakfast is not to be sniffed at! Finally, just to prove that ghosts aren't exclusive to old houses and pubs, we learn of the revenant that haunts a runway at Heathrow Airport.

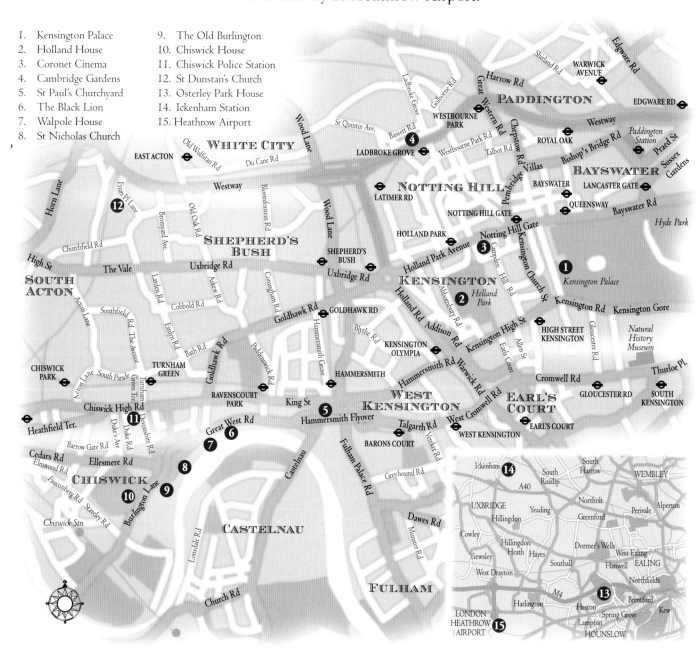

KENSINGTON PALACE
KENSINGTON GARDENS, W8
Why Don't They Come?

Beginning life as a Jacobean mansion, this house became a royal palace in 1689, when William III (1650–1702) bought it in the hope that its pastoral location would alleviate his chronic asthma. Architects Sir Christopher Wren and Nicholas Hawksmoor subsequently renovated the building and, following William's death, Queen Anne (1665–1714), who died here from an attack of apoplexy brought on by overeating, lived here. George I (1660–1727) and George II (1683–1760), all chose Kensington Palace as their favoured London residence. George II's last days were spent at Kensington Palace, anxiously awaiting long overdue dispatches from Hanover. Hour after hour, he would cast a hopeful glance up at the weather vane that stood over the entrance, hoping to see the wind change direction and speed his messengers to him. His courtiers would often hear his agitated voice sounding from his chamber, as he called out in his broken, heavily accented English: 'Why don't they come?' His wishes remained unfulfilled for, by the time the wind did change direction, the king had died. However, his ghost still returns to the palace, where his fretful face often appears at the window of his chamber, gazing up towards the weather vane. And every so often his voice is heard echoing along the corridors crying: 'Why don't they come?'

During the reign of George III (1738–1820), several members of the royal family lived at Kensington Palace, among them the king's fifth daughter, Princess Sophia. She fell deeply in love with a royal equerry, Thomas Garth, and bore him an illegitimate son. No sooner had she given birth, than Garth's ardour waned and poor Sophia retreated into a reclusive existence in her apartments at Kensington Palace. As the years passed, her eyesight began to fail, and her only solace in her old age was to sit at her spinning wheel or toil at her embroidery frame. Although she died at nearby York House, her spirit returns to Kensington Palace, where the sound of a ghostly spinning wheel, cranked

ABOVE: The ghost of George II still calls for news of despatches from Hanover at Kensington Palace.

PREVIOUS PAGE: Although it is now a youth hostel a headless spectre still wanders through the rooms of Holland House.

by an invisible hand has been heard creaking in the early hours of some mornings.

HOLLAND HOUSE
HOLLAND PARK, W11
Three Drops of Ghostly Blood

Although devastated by bombing in World War II enough of its façade has survived to remind us of what a fairytale place Holland House must have been. It was built in 1606 for Sir Walter Cope, Chancellor of the Exchequer to James I. In his will, Cope left the house to his wife, on condition that she did not remarry. When she did, the house passed to their daughter Lady Rich, whose husband was created Earl of Holland in 1624. He was beheaded for his royalist sympathies during the Civil War. The house was later restored to Lady Holland and was passed down through successive generations of the family until Henry Fox, 1st Baron Holland, purchased it in 1763. It was during the tenure of the 3rd Baron Holland that the glory days of Holland House commenced. His wife, Elizabeth Vassall, entertained an impressive selection of the great, good and infamous at their house, including William IV, Lord Byron, Benjamin Disraeli and Lord Macaulay, to name but a few. Charles Dickens, who became a close friend, was once moved to wonder who would take the place of these rare personalities when they had 'stepped into the shadow'.

Today the King George Memorial Youth Hostel occupies what remains of the building, but the ghost of the 1st Earl of Holland has been known to walk its corridors, just as he did the rooms of Holland House. In the past the earl's appearances were presaged by three drops of blood, which appeared alongside a hidden door. Then, as the clock chimed midnight, his phantom materialized from within the hidden recess, his head tucked firmly under his arm. Drifting his way about the building he surveyed the rooms and corridors of his old home, until as the first rays of dawn stretched across the grounds, the earl returned to the hidden door to fade away once more.

ABOVE: Despite extensive bomb damage, enough of Holland House survives to give an impression of what it was like in the days when Dickens came calling.

CORONET CINEMA
103 NOTTING HILL GATE, W11
The Cashier Who Fell from Grace

Boasting one of London's most glorious cinema interiors, the Coronet is a true survivor whose majestic Art Nouveau interior is strangely at odds with the Hollywood blockbusters that flicker across its screen today. In the early 1900s the building was a successful and popular theatre, and it was around this time that it acquired its ghostly resident. Tradition holds that one of the cashiers was caught with her fingers in the till and that when she was called into the manager's office to be confronted with her crime, she let out a scream of despair and raced from the room. She then ran for all she was worth up the stairs to the upper circle, where she flung herself from the balcony and plunged to her death in the well of the theatre below. Thereafter the woman's wraith remained to chill the blood of those who worked at the theatre. Indeed, when staff meetings were held in the upper levels of the building,

her ghost caused so much disruption that the management was obliged to transfer these meetings to the lower levels. Agitated footsteps have also been heard racing up the stairs towards the balcony from which, long ago, she took her plunge into the hereafter. Since the tragic event occurred at Christmas, it is during the festive period that the ghostly activity most often occurs.

CAMBRIDGE GARDENS
NOTTING HILL GATE, W11
The Phantom Bus

There can be few hauntings that are as bizarre and dramatic as that which afflicts Cambridge Gardens in the early hours of some mornings. The phantom in question is that of a number seven double-decker London bus, which was last seen in May 1990. However, it first came to public attention early one morning in 1934, when a motorist driving along Cambridge Gardens suddenly swerved for no apparent reason, and was killed as his car hit a wall and burst into flames. At the subsequent inquest into the driver's death, witnesses came forward to testify to the existence of a phantom bus, which many of them had seen in more or less the exact spot where the fatal crash had occurred. They told how it would always appear at about 1.15 a.m. (the time that the crash had occurred) and they spoke of their terror as it came racing along the centre of the road towards them. No driver was ever visible in the bus, and no lights were ever on. Convinced that they were about to experience a head-on collision with the vehicle, motorists would swerve out of its path, and the bus would thunder past them. However, whenever they turned around to look at the bus, they always found that it had vanished without trace.

St Paul's Churchyard
Queen Caroline Street, Hammersmith, W6
The Ghost of Regular Habits

This late 19th-century, Gothic-style church cowers somewhat uneasily alongside the Hammersmith flyover. Although its churchyard was long ago grassed over, a few old tombs, along with a handful of gravestones, still survive, and it is around these weathered memorials that the Hammersmith ghost is

BELOW: The ghost of Barbara Villiers, Duchess of Cleveland still laments the loss of her looks at Chiswick's Walpole House despite the passage of almost 300 years.

said to appear every 50 years. A report in the *West London Observer* in July 1955 informed readers that the spectre was due to make an appearance the following Wednesday night. This announcement caused something of a local sensation, and 400 people turned up in the hope of encountering the apparition. One elderly resident, who had seen the ghost in 1905, promised that it would be wearing 'a white winding sheet, its eyes flaming'.

On the night in question, despite the fact that the police had sealed off the churchyard, a few hoaxers managed to slip through the cordon and were able to amuse the crowd with their ghostly impersonations. But when midnight came and went without so much as a drop in temperature, the crowd grew bored and quickly dispersed. Fortunately, the *West London Observer* reporter and a few hardy souls opted to maintain their vigil, and at about 1 a.m. their endeavour was rewarded. A legless figure clad in brilliant white, glided from the church porch and drifted silently towards the tomb where sundry members of the Fenn and Colvill families lay buried. The spectators watched, open mouthed, as the figure floated onto the tomb and promptly melted into it. Other witnesses, who had seen the entire episode from a window overlooking the churchyard, observed how a strange wind had rustled the branches of the trees shortly before the ghost had appeared. Local residents will soon have a potential opportunity to witness the Hammersmith Ghost, for its next scheduled appearance is due in July 2005.

The Black Lion
2 South Black Lion Lane, Hammersmith, W6
The Hammersmith Ghost

In 1803, Black Lion Lane and the surrounding area were much troubled by appearances of the so-called 'Hammersmith Ghost', a fearsome phantom that emerged from the shadows to moan, wail and writhe before terrified witnesses. On one occasion a pregnant woman was so shocked by the phantom that she died within two days of encountering it. Another appearance by the spectre caused a waggoner to leap from his vehicle in fright, much to the consternation of his 16 passengers who were almost killed when the horses bolted. By January 1804, the ghost's nocturnal activities held the area in a grip of terror, and so a local excise officer called Francis Smith decided to do something about the situation. One night, having 'filled his blunderbuss with shot, and himself with ale', Smith set out to hunt down the fearsome spectre. Unfortunately he mistakenly shot dead a white-clothed plasterer called Thomas Millwood who was innocently making his way home from work. The subsequent inquest was held at The Black Lion pub, located at the end of the lane in which the tragedy had occurred. A verdict of wilful murder was returned against Francis Smith and at his subsequent trial at the Old Bailey he was found guilty and sentenced to be hanged. However, given the extenuating circumstances of his crime, a stay of execution was granted and his sentence was later commuted to just one year in prison.

Meanwhile the tragedy had spurred the relatives of the real ghost into bringing him to notice. It transpired that he was a shoemaker named Graham whose motivation was to wreak revenge on his apprentices, who had terrified his children by telling them ghost stories. As *The Times* explained: 'He expected to check them of this disagreeable bent of their minds to the prejudice of his children, by presenting them as they passed homewards, a figure of a ghost', which, it seems, he managed very successfully.

WALPOLE HOUSE
CHISWICK MALL, W4
She Longs Eternally

This handsome 16th-century building was renovated in the 17th century and its handsome brick façade was added in 1730. Past residents have included the Irish politician Daniel O'Connell (1775–1847), who lodged here from 1794 to 1795 whilst studying law in London, and author William Makepeace Thackeray (1811–63) who attended Mrs Ockerby's academy for young gentlemen here in the early 19th century. Thackeray later immortalized the house as Miss Pinkerton's Academy in his novel *Vanity Fair*. However, it is the ghost of an earlier resident, Barbara Villiers, Lady Castlemaine, which is said to haunt the building. Barbara Villiers (1641–1709), who was created Duchess of Cleveland in 1670, was one of the greatest beauties of the 17th century, and as such attracted the roving eye of King Charles II (1630–85), becoming his mistress and bearing him three sons and two daughters. Diarist Samuel Pepys called her 'the curse of the nation', yet when he dreamt one night of holding her in his arms he commented that, if death meant slipping into such a dreamlike existence, it wouldn't be too bad!

However, by the time the duchess came to live at Walpole House in 1705, her royal lover was long dead, and her appearance had begun to change alarmingly. She had swollen 'gradually to a monstrous bulk', which her physicians diagnosed

ABOVE: Barbara Villiers still stands by the windows of Chiswick's Walpole House imploring her maker to restore her beauty.

as dropsy (a disease in which the body retains large amounts of fluid), and the two years she spent here proved to be the most miserable of her life. Local residents spoke of seeing her standing at the windows, bathed in moonlight, her hands clasped to her breast, imploring God to restore her beauty. But her pleas went unanswered, the dropsy proved incurable and on Sunday 9th October, 1709, the Duchess of Cleveland died at the age of 67.

Her lament at the loss of her beauty appears to have lingered on. For many is the time that people walking along Chiswick Mall on nights when the Moon is full, have spied the puffy, bloated face of Barbara Villiers pressed against the glass of Walpole House, her dark eyes rolling in despair, as her restless wraith pursues its eternal quest for the restoration of her long-lost looks.

St Nicholas Church
CHURCH STREET, CHISWICK, W4
The Ladies of Illustrious Birth

Founded in the 15th-century, this church's dedication to St Nicholas, the patron saint of sailors and fishermen, remembers the days when Chiswick was a busy riverside fishing village. Although the main body of the church was rebuilt in 1882, the tower remains much as it was 500 years ago. Amongst those buried in its churchyard are painter and engraver, William Hogarth (1697–1764), artist J. M. Whistler (1834–1903), and Barbara Villiers, Duchess of Cleveland (1641–1709, see page 85). Meanwhile, Mary Fauconberg and Frances Rich, daughters of Oliver Cromwell (1599–1658), lie buried in a vault beneath the church's chancel, along with — so rumour has it — the remains of their father.

It has long been suspected that following Oliver Cromwell's posthumous beheading (see page 32), Mary Fauconberg brought his body to Chiswick, having bribed a guard to let her smuggle her father's headless cadaver away from Tyburn. Here Cromwell was secretly interred in the vault in which Mary and her sister would eventually be buried. During the rebuilding of the church in 1882, their vault was opened in order to see if there was any veracity in the rumours surrounding Cromwell's final resting place. Captain Dale, the then vicar's son, claimed that, along with the coffins of the two sisters, he spied a third coffin, which showed signs of rough usage, and was pushed hard against the far side of the vault. Cromwell's name still aroused violent emotion at the time, so the vicar, fearing the arrival of groups of sightseers to moralize over the Lord Protector, had the vault bricked up and left unmarked. Perhaps it is the fact that their resting place was desecrated by a clergyman, who by his own admission resented everything their father stood for, which has caused the ghosts of the two ladies to roam the churchyard in the hours before dawn. Their white-clad figures drift silently amongst the graves, until, with the coming of the first light of day, they melt slowly into the fabric of the church and return to their unmarked grave.

The Old Burlington
POWELL'S WALK, CHISWICK, W4
The Eternal Tippler

Standing opposite St Nicholas Church, the Old Burlington is a beautiful Elizabethan building that was once a famous inn

ABOVE: Is it possible that Oliver Cromwell lies buried in a secret location at St Nicholas Church in Chiswick?
LEFT: The Old Burlington has changed little since the days when it was a lively tavern visited by the likes of Dick Turpin.

known as the Burlington Arms. It boasts four front doors, outside one of which you can still see an old cupboard where inebriated patrons used to be incarcerated for the night. Dick Turpin is said to have enjoyed his wedding breakfast here, and legend maintains that on another occasion, the authorities spotted the highwayman's horse tied up outside the inn and hammered on the door, intent on bringing him to justice. However, Turpin outwitted his pursuers by leaping onto his mount from an upstairs window and galloping away as they searched for him inside the inn. Although the building has now been converted into two private dwellings, two ghosts from its past are still said to wander the premises. One is a young girl dressed in a black skirt with a high waist and a poke bonnet. The other is a man in dark clothing, wearing a swirling cloak and a wide-brimmed hat, whom successive residents have come to know as 'Percy'. Both are harmless spectres, who do little more than stare out from the windows, content to watch the world go by, although which world they are watching, is a matter of some conjecture.

CHISWICK HOUSE
BURLINGTON LANE, CHISWICK, W4
The Phantom Breakfast

Modelled on Palladio's Villa Rotonda in Vicenza, Italy, and surrounded by peaceful, landscaped grounds, Chiswick House was designed by Richard Boyle (1695–1753), the 3rd Earl of Burlington and built between 1725 and 1729. The remarkable building stands as a monument to his appreciation of the arts. Boyle lived in an adjoining Jacobean mansion, which was demolished in 1758, and used the new house to exhibit his works of art and to entertain friends, including the composer George Frideric Handel (1695–1759), the poet Alexander Pope (1688–1744) and the writer Jonathan Swift (1667–1745). The house later came into the ownership of various Dukes of Devonshire. Whig Statesman and Foreign Secretary, Charles James Fox (1749–1806) died here, as did Prime Minister George Canning (1770–1827). In 1892 the 8th Duke of Devonshire moved to Chatsworth in Derbyshire, and Chiswick House became a private mental asylum. Middlesex County Council purchased the building in 1929 and, over the next 30 years, it was allowed to fall into disrepair.

In 1958 the Ministry of Works began an extensive restoration project, aiming to restore the house to its former glory. As the workmen set about their task, they appear to have disturbed the spirits of several former residents. The aroma of bacon and eggs, which the workmen attributed to the ghost of 'one of the mad cooks', often wafted around the building, despite the fact that no cooking ever took place in the vicinity. Although the restoration was completed long ago, staff and visitors are still mystified by the distinctive smell of fried bacon that sometimes permeates the air in the back gallery. It can hang in the air for several months at a time, and then not be noticed for a few years. Elsewhere in the house, visitors have sensed a female presence in the bedchamber. On one occasion a woman was admiring the mirror in the room – it is the only original

BELOW: The daughters of Oliver Cromwell, swathed in white, wander amongst the graves of Chiswick's St Nicholas churchyard.

death by her son-in-law, Thomas Wainwright. Chiswick Fire Station occupied the site originally, and on several occasions firemen were startled to hear the distinct sound of a woman's footsteps walking briskly across the basement in the dead of night. What was particularly unsettling was the fact that should anyone venture into the basement to investigate, the footfall stopped abruptly as the door was opened. Although this particular phenomenon has not been repeated since the police force have occupied the building, there have been reports of a spectral lady dressed in blue who, in the early hours of some mornings, has flitted past the boys in blue on the third floor of the building.

ABOVE: The ghostly aroma of fried bacon is often smelt at the elegant Chiswick House.

mirror in the house — and was startled by the distinctive reflection of Lady Burlington standing behind her. However, when she turned around, the woman found that her spectral companion was nowhere to be seen.

CHISWICK POLICE STATION
209–211 CHISWICK HIGH ROAD, W4
Mrs Abercrombie's Spectral Return

The squat, modern building that houses Chiswick Police Station, stands on the site of Linden House, an 18th-century manor where, in 1792, a Mrs Abercrombie was hacked to

ST DUNSTAN'S CHURCH
EAST ACTON, W3
The Colour-changing Monks

During the middle ages a monastery stood on the site now occupied by St Dunstan's Church, which may account for the ghostly monks that have been known to manifest themselves before astonished witnesses in sundry locations about the building. The Reverend Anton-Stevens, who began his tenure at the church in 1944, and who died in 1966, regularly saw a procession of phantom friars wearing brown habits, their hoods pulled up over their heads, drifting along the central aisle towards the altar. He even claimed to have spoken at length with one of the monks, who obligingly dictated an article, which Anton-Stevens subsequently published in the parish magazine.

Kenneth Mason, a reporter with the *Daily Graphic*, was determined to discover whether the church was haunted or not and spent a November evening inside the building. However, he found the vigil so boring that he fell fast asleep. He awoke with a start to find six monks — this time in grey habits — walking towards him along the central aisle. Anxious for a scoop, the fearless reporter rose from his pew and stood right in their path. Unperturbed, the ghostly procession simply walked right through him!

OSTERLEY PARK HOUSE
JERSEY ROAD, ISLEWORTH, MIDDLESEX, TW7
The White Lady of Osterley

Although the Elizabethan financial magnate Sir Thomas Gresham (1519–79) built the original Tudor manor house at Osterley Park in about 1562, it was the 18th-century acquisition of the estate by the founders of Child's Bank, which saw the building transformed into the splendid palatial property that today nestles amidst a tranquil landscape of woods, lakes and fields.

The house is haunted by the elegant spectre of a beautiful lady in a flowing white dress. Little is known about either her origins, or her reason for roaming the property, but her favoured time for appearing is around 4.30 p.m. Over the years she has been seen by workmen employed on the maintenance of the property, and by casual visitors who happen to chance upon her and are most put out by her sudden disappearances. In 1978 three children on a school outing to Osterley Park saw her. They told their teachers how a lady had appeared in an archway by the main stairs and had proceeded to drift out of sight, although there was no doorway in the vicinity where she had, apparently, vanished. It was only when the teachers questioned staff at the house that they learnt of the existence of the mysterious 'White Lady' and were then able to explain to their charges how they had been just one of a long line of people whom she had graced with an appearance.

ABOVE: Stop in at East Acton's St Dunstan's church and a group of ghostly friars may be there to welcome you.

ICKENHAM STATION
ICKENHAM, MIDDLESEX, UB10
She Fell from the Platform

In the early hours of one morning in 1951 an electrician working on the platform at Ickenham Station glanced up to find a middle-aged woman in a red scarf standing over him, watching his every move. Suddenly she raised her hand and beckoned him to follow her. He felt himself strangely compelled to do so, and trekked obediently behind her, across the platform and down one of the staircases. But the moment her foot touched the bottom stair, the woman vanished into thin air, leaving the nonplussed workman to race off and report his strange encounter to the station manager. The electrician discovered that, far from this being an isolated incident, many station workers had reported similar sightings of the mysterious woman. It is believed that she is the ghost of a lady who fell from the platform onto the rails long ago, and received a fatal electric shock.

HEATHROW AIRPORT
The Ghost on Runway 1

Although historic old houses, atmospheric churches and snug inns are the most conducive places in which spectres can roam, modern buildings and institutions are not immune to ghostly goings on. An airport runway might seem to be an unlikely place for a haunting, but on Heathrow's Runway 1, there have been sightings of a tall man, dressed in twill cavalry trousers and wearing a bowler hat. Tradition holds that he is the ghost of one of the passengers aboard a DC3 aircraft that crashed onto the runway on 2nd March, 1948, killing everyone on board. Shortly after the accident, a mysterious man, dressed in the aforementioned style, allegedly approached the rescue workers, and enquired politely if they had found his briefcase. Moments later, he had disappeared and no trace of him could be found.

NORTH LONDON

WILDERNESS AND BYGONE AMBIENCE are to be found to the north of London. There is the bracing expanse of Hampstead Heath which offers the intrepid seeker after the unknown the opportunity to encounter a galloping horseman. Venturing in to the lovely village of Hampstead, you can seek out several historic though haunted pubs. Nearby in the village of Highgate, prepare to have your marrow chilled as you wander among the crumbling tombs of the vast necropolis of Highgate Cemetery.

1. The Camden Brewing Company
2. William IV
3. The Flask Tavern
4. Holly Bush
5. East Heath Road
6. Hampstead Ponds and Hampstead Heath
7. The Spaniards Inn
8. Highgate Cemetery
9. The Flask
10. Pond Square
11. The Gatehouse
12. Bruce Castle
13. Barnet Road
14. Enfield Chace
15. Rose and Crown
16. Bell Lane

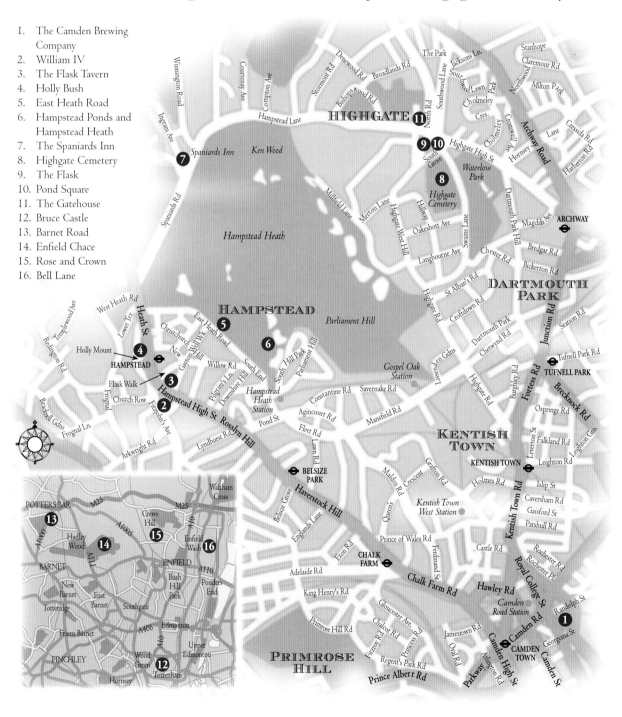

THE CAMDEN BREWING COMPANY
1 RANDOLPH STREET, NW1
The Ghostly Duellist

In July 1843, Colonel Fawcett was mortally wounded in one of London's last traditional duels. The dying man was carried to the Camden Arms Inn, where he died in a pool of his own blood. Tradition has it that his tormented soul has remained in limbo ever since, trapped at the spot where he breathed his last breath. The Camden Brewing Company pub now occupies the site of the Camden Arms, and there have been frequent reports of Fawcett's ghost hovering around the listed spiral staircase that stands at the back of the building and on which the unfortunate duellist is thought to have died. His spectral ramblings have dwindled considerably in the last six years or so. Indeed, landlady Lesley Ridgeway bemoaned the fact that although 'we've had a few people come in… talking about this so-called ghost… I've never seen anything… he seems to have vanished into thin air.' However, pub expert Mike Lewis of the

BELOW: The ghost of a suicide victim has been known to leap from the upper levels of Bruce Castle, once the home of postal reformer Roland Hill.

North London Campaign for Real Ale proved reluctant to assign the ghost to the pages of history. 'Just because he hasn't been seen for a while,' he told the *Highbury and Islington Gazette*, 'doesn't mean he's not there.'

WILLIAM IV
77 HAMPSTEAD HIGH STREET, NW3
The Tooth Is Out There

Peering down onto Hampstead High Street, the William IV pub is a cosy little place that was once the house of a local doctor, so tradition claims. For reasons long since forgotten, the medic murdered his wife, and bricked up her body in a recess in the basement of the house, a room that is now the pub's cellar. Not much pleased by this, the spirit of the doctor's wife still makes its displeasure known by rattling windows and slamming doors in the dead of night.

Meanwhile, people walking past the pub have glimpsed the poignant shade of a young girl, standing on tiptoes and gazing anxiously through the windows of the pub. She is swathed in a white shroud, and her long, plaited hair hangs untidily across her shoulder. Few people can fail to have sympathy for the plight that left this poor girl's spirit earthbound. Most versions of her tale agree that, some time early in the 20th century, the girl's parents left her at a dentist's surgery that once stood opposite the William IV and then crossed over to the pub, leaving their daughter to endure the ordeal alone. So traumatic did the girl find the experience that she killed herself rather than keep her next dentist's appointment. From time to time ever since, her ghost has been seen peeping in at the windows of the William IV, seeking the parents who, not content with leaving her to face the whining terror of the dentist's drill alone, have apparently also abandoned her to face eternity by herself.

'JUST BECAUSE HE HASN'T BEEN SEEN FOR A WHILE, DOES NOT MEAN HE'S NOT THERE'

THE PHANTOM DUELLIST

THE FLASK TAVERN
14 FLASK WALK, HAMPSTEAD, NW3
Monty Keeps a Watchful Eye

Tucked away at the end of a pedestrian thoroughfare that leads from Hampstead High Street, the Flask Tavern is very much a pub for locals. Its name recalls the days in the 18th century when Hampstead attempted to re-invent itself as a spa village, and people trekked up from the City of London to take the waters at its Chalybeate Wells. Anxious to capitalize on the passing trade, the landlord of the pub began selling flasks to those visiting the spa, and thus the pub acquired its name. The ghost of a 19th-century landlord, whom tradition remembers as 'Monty', haunts the hostelry. Nobody really knows much about his living self, but in death his revenant is something of a stickler for tradition, and likes to keep an eye on those who are now entrusted with the running of his pub. Monty finds change particularly irksome, and he was moved to spectral indignation by the redevelopment of the Flask's conservatory in 1997. He disrupted work as often as he could by hiding the workmen's tools and switching off plugs. Once the building work was complete, the ghostly landlord continued to disturb the pub, frequently interrupting

BELOW: Monty the 19th-century landlord likes to keep a ghostly eye on the comings and goings at his pub, The Flask in Hampstead.

customers' meals by moving tables across the floor in front of them. However, Monty appears to have bowed to the inevitable more recently, and has grown to accept the new conservatory, becoming relatively inactive.

HOLLY BUSH
22 HOLLY MOUNT, HAMPSTEAD, NW3
The Phantom Waitress

If you come to lunch in the gas-lit, 18th-century Holly Bush Inn, and find your order being taken by a polite, efficient waitress, wearing a crisp, white, linen apron over a long, dark skirt, do not be surprised if your meal never arrives. 'We don't offer waitress service,' says Peter Dures, who, with his wife Hazel, ran the pub during the mid-1990s, would explain wearily to irate customers who had stormed up to the bar demanding to know why their meals were taking so long. 'But we gave our order to a waitress,' these patrons insisted invariably. 'Then I'm sorry,' Peter would reply, 'but you've given your order to our ghost!' Nobody knows whom she was or is, and nobody knows why she has this compunction to come back and wait on tables in death. But come back she does, and no one can fault her, as she is extremely courteous as she takes an order. The one thing she doesn't do, however, is to deliver your order to the kitchen so that you can get your meal!

In the late 1950s, a resident jazz band used to perform at the Holly Bush on Sunday nights. The bandleader always finished his set by walking off the tiny dais on which he had been performing, slapping the pianist on the back as he walked past. Peter and Hazel resurrected the inn's musical tradition, only to find that their piano player was often rewarded with a phantom slap on his back.

EAST HEATH ROAD
HAMPSTEAD, NW3
The Phantom Cyclist

East Heath Road runs alongside the western fringe of Hampstead Heath and has an untamed and delightfully rural quality about it. On cold winter nights, as twilight creeps

ABOVE: Those who swim in the murky waters of Hampstead Ponds speak of chilling footsteps following them around.

across the heath, and the towering trees that line the road dapple the pavement in sinister shadow, a leering, toothless old man, dressed in a brown Norfolk jacket, has been known to follow unwary pedestrians. The experience is particularly unnerving, as he appears to be very real. Indeed, the first hint that anyone has that he is anything other than flesh and blood is when they turn around to look at him, and he vanishes abruptly before their eyes!

HAMPSTEAD PONDS AND HAMPSTEAD HEATH, NW3
The Horseman's Shadow

Hampstead Heath is comprised of 800 acres of wild and rugged moorland, which as well as being a playground for generations of Londoners, also provides a lush habitat for an abundance of wildlife. Yet in parts the heath is a sinister place, with towering trees casting its rough pathways into ethereal shadow. Numerous ponds dot the heath and hardy swimmers make use of several of them frequently. Some of these swimmers complain of hearing phantom footsteps

OPPOSITE: Take the tour of old Highgate Cemetery and be prepared for a sinister wander in the realm of vampires.

BELOW: The Spaniards Inn in Hampstead is one of the many, many pubs to claim Dick Turpin's ghost as an ethereal regular.

following them along the jetties as they prepare to leap into the cold, murky waters. No explanation has ever been found as to who – or what – might be responsible for the footsteps, although several witnesses believe them to be connected with suicides that, in the past, chose to end their lives in the ponds.

The open spaces of the heath afford little protection from the malevolent forces that lurk hereabouts. In the 17th and 18th centuries, the rugged paths that cross its untamed wilderness were the haunt of numerous highwaymen, the so-called 'Gentlemen of the Road', who would stop at nothing to relieve travellers of their possessions and even their lives.

It would seem that one such felon found the lure of the heath so irresistible that he is loath to leave it. Over the years there have been numerous reports of a dark figure on horseback, which comes riding from the dense thickets and gallops towards astonished witnesses. One woman who encountered the phantom told how she was so convinced that she was about to be trampled to death that she flung herself to the ground and prepared for the impact. After a few moments, she looked up to find that the ghostly rider and his mount had apparently vanished into thin air. Only then did it dawn on her that, despite the fact that they were coming towards her at great speed, the horse's hooves had not made the slightest sound upon the hard ground.

THE SPANIARDS INN
SPANIARDS ROAD, HAMPSTEAD HEATH, NW3
Turpin's Cosy Lair

The 16th-century Spaniards Inn stands on the edge of Hampstead Heath and is as pleasant a hostelry as you could ever wish to encounter. It is a low-beamed, atmospheric old place, reputedly named for two Spanish brothers who both fell in love with the same woman and then killed each other in a duel. During the Gordon Riots of 1780, the rioters stopped off at the inn on their way to destroy nearby Kenwood

House, which was then the home of the Earl of Mansfield. The quick-thinking landlord assured the rioters of his loyalty to their cause and to demonstrate his solidarity offered them unlimited refreshments. Thus was he able to stall them until military aid arrived and the destruction of Kenwood was prevented.

That the inn was also a favoured haunt of Dick Turpin, who is commemorated by the snug Turpin Bar on the first floor, where a warming log fire crackles in an ancient hearth in the winter months. Customers enjoying a quiet pint in this particular room have experienced the mysterious sensation of having their sleeves tugged by an invisible hand. In the downstairs bar, meanwhile, a shadowy cloaked figure – who some believe to be Turpin himself – has been known to stride purposefully across the bar before vanishing abruptly into the wall near the toilets.

HIGHGATE CEMETERY
SWAINS LANE, HIGHGATE, N6
The City of the Dead

Sprawling across 20 acres of grassy hillside, Highgate Cemetery opened in 1839, and quickly became the most sought-after burial ground in London: indeed the fashion-conscious Victorians would not be seen dead in any other cemetery. By the beginning of the 20th century, tens of thousands of people had been laid to rest in its hallowed ground, including many famous and illustrious names. The cemetery's monuments to the dead became ever more ambitious as families struggled desperately to outdo one another by providing increasingly ostentatious resting places for their loved ones.

However, as the dark days of World War II descended upon the capital, the cemetery's fortunes suffered a severe downturn, and by the 1960s this once-proud necropolis had been abandoned. Decay and neglect crept unchecked amongst the tombs, as the roots of advancing vegetation wrenched the magnificent graves apart, leaving their twisted masonry sprawled across toppled columns.

Rumours were soon circulating of sinister cults holding strange ceremonies in the abandoned ruins after dark. Then, the local newspaper, the *Hampstead and Highgate Express*, began to receive letters from frightened readers telling of ghostly encounters around the cemetery. One man, whose car had broken down nearby, was terrified by a hideous apparition with glowing red eyes, glaring at him through the rusting iron gates. Another man walking along the dark and forbidding Swain's Lane, found himself suddenly knocked to the ground by a fearsome creature that 'seemed to glide' from the wall of the cemetery. He was only saved from the monster when the headlights of an approaching car seemed to cause the thing to dissolve into thin air.

When it was subsequently suggested that a vampire might be loose in the old cemetery the hunt for the un-dead was underway, as a veritable barrage of journalists, camera crews, eager occultists and the just plain curious, swarmed around the grim, decaying mausoleums, garlic and crucifixes at the ready.

Meanwhile letters telling of frightening encounters in the vicinity of Swain's Lane continued to grace the pages of the local press. A ghostly cyclist, puffing his way up the steep incline had terrified one young mother, whilst other unfortunate locals had witnessed a tall man in a top hat, strolling nonchalantly across the road before disappearing into the wall of the cemetery. His nebulous stroll was always accompanied by a mournful tolling from the bells in the old, disused chapel.

In the 1980s, a massive restoration project by the enthusiastic 'Friends of Highgate Cemetery' went some way to reversing the neglect of the previous decades. As they cleared the pathways and uncovered many of the spectacular tombs the ghostly activity began to recede. Today, spectral sightings are reduced to just two figures. One is the ghost of a mad old woman, her long grey hair streaming behind her as she races amongst the graves, searching for her children, whom she is supposed to have murdered in a fit of insane rage. The other is a shrouded figure who gazes pensively into space, seemingly oblivious to the presence of witnesses, until they get too close, whereupon it vanishes, only to reappear a short distance away, adopting the same meditative pose.

and its link to the haunting is somewhat tenuous, to say the least. However, the staff knows when her ghost is about to honour them with a visit, because her appearances are presaged by a sudden and alarming drop in temperature. A full-blown manifestation is a rare occurrence, but lights certainly begin to sway back and forth mysteriously, glasses are moved across tables in front of surprised customers, and some people even suffer the alarming sensation of feeling her invisible form blowing gently down the backs of their necks.

POND SQUARE
HIGHGATE, N6
The Ghostly Chicken

Although the water source from which it derives its name was filled in 1864, Pond Square still has a certain charm. Massive plane trees cast long shadows across the asphalt, and the chance of an encounter with one of London's most unusual spectres certainly enhances its ambience.

Sir Francis Bacon, (1561–1626) was a politician, writer and philosopher who also dabbled in scientific experiments. He was one of the first people to propagate the theory that refrigeration might be utilized as a means of preserving meat. One bitterly cold morning in January 1626, whilst in the company of his good friend Dr Winterbourne, Bacon decided to put his theory to the test by purchasing a chicken from an old woman on Highgate Hill. Having slaughtered and plucked the bird, he stuffed its carcass with snow. By a deliciously ironic twist of fate, Sir Francis caught a severe chill as a result of his experiment. He was taken to nearby Arundel House where he was placed in a damp bed, but he died shortly afterwards.

Ever since Bacon's death, there have been frequent reports of a phantom white bird, resembling a plucked chicken, which appears from nowhere to race round Pond Square in frenzied circles, flapping its wings as it runs. In 1943, one Terence Long was crossing the square late at night when he heard the sound of horses hooves accompanied by the low rumble of carriage wheels. Suddenly, a raucous shriek split the silence, and the ghostly chicken appeared before him. It proceeded to race around frantically, before vanishing into thin air. In the 1960s a motorist, whose car had broken down close by, encountered the same apparition, as did a courting couple in the 1970s, when the chicken interrupted their passionate encounter by dropping suddenly from above and landing next to them! In recent years, however, sightings of the featherless phantom have been few and far between. Indeed, it might just be possible that its restless spirit has finally accepted the indecency of its demise, and the scientific principle for which it gave its life!

ABOVE: Highgate's Pond Square might not be particularly noteworthy but the phantom chicken that haunts it most certainly is.

THE FLASK
77 HIGHGATE WEST HILL, HIGHGATE, N6
The Bullet in the Wall

The 18th-century Flask is one of Highgate's most atmospheric pubs. It was once patronized by the artist William Hogarth (1697–1764), whom, it is said, once produced an instant sketch of a fight, which he witnessed on the premises between two customers who set about each other with their beer tankards. The ghost of a female phantom haunts the pub, although nobody is certain of her identity. Some claim that she is the ghost of one of the pub's former maidservants, who committed suicide when an illicit romance went sour. Others maintain that her apparition is connected with a bullet that is embedded in the wall of the snug bar to the right of the entrance. Nobody is certain when, why or at whom the bullet was fired

THE GATEHOUSE
1 NORTH ROAD, HIGHGATE, N6
The Ghostly Presence

This rambling, part-timbered pub, which was rebuilt in 1905, is named after the gateway at which travellers once paid their tolls to cross land that was owned by the Bishop of London. Indeed it was this 'high gate' that gave its name to the area. Several ghosts are believed to haunt The Gatehouse. The best known is that of Mother Marnes, who in life was an old woman who was murdered for her meagre life savings in the original gatehouse. She is a selective spirit, as she only ever appears when there are no children or animals on the premises. One night in the 1960s, the childless, single landlord of the time, went up to the minstrels' gallery and was attacked by 'something' that came at him from the shadows. 'I had gone up to switch off the gallery lights,' he recalled, 'when all of a sudden this thing appeared from nowhere. I can remember nothing else until waking up in hospital.' However, no sooner had the landlord recovered and returned to the pub, than he was attacked by the entity again. So terrified was the man that he requested a transfer.

The minstrels' gallery has since been converted into a pleasant little pub theatre. When landlord John Plews and his staff cleared out the room, they threw out years of accumulated junk, with the exception of a heavy table, which they left in the centre of the room. On several occasions, John and his staff unlocked the door in the mornings to find that the table had been mysteriously moved across the room and placed under the window during the night. Despite a thorough investigation, John never discovered any logical reason for the table's movement, and concluded that it must have been the ghost enjoying a spectral prank.

BRUCE CASTLE
LORDSHIP LANE, TOTTENHAM, N17
The Melancholic Shade of Lady Coleraine

Tradition holds that this Tudor manor house, which was once the home of postal reformer Sir Rowland Hill (1795–1879), stands on the site of a castle built by the father of Robert the Bruce. The manor certainly did once belong to the Scottish Royal family. Above the clock on the exterior of the building, the window of a small chamber can be seen. It was in this room that the 2nd Lord Coleraine (1636–1708) is said to have imprisoned his beautiful wife, Constantia, and their infant, for fear that anyone else should gaze upon her. Distraught at her detention the poor lady was finally overcome by grief, and on 3rd November, 1680, Constantia took her baby in her arms and leapt from the balustrade, crashing on to the paving stones below. Her disturbing screams echoed down the centuries, and were heard on the anniversary of her death each year. However, in the early years of the

BELOW: Tottenham's Bruce Castle was, so tradition maintains, once the site of a castle owned by the father of Robert the Bruce.

20th century a sympathetic clergyman took pity on her agonized spirit and held a prayer service in her room in the hope of laying it to rest. Although he managed to quell the woman's screams, her silent shade occasionally repeats her suicide, much to the consternation of astonished passers-by.

In July 1971, two people walking past the building late one night noticed a group of revellers in 18th-century costume, who were apparently enjoying a ball. What caught their attention was the fact that these strangely attired guests were making no sound and appeared to be floating in mid-air. A few days later, another couple saw the same mysterious figures and approached them to enquire what was happening, whereupon the figures slowly melted into thin air …

BARNET ROAD
ENFIELD, EN6
The Murder Victim Who Can Never Rest

The sun was setting and the autumn night was closing in as Mr Ward and his uncle travelled home along the Enfield to Barnet road. All was quiet and still, the only sound being the clatter of the horses' hooves and the low rumble of the carriage wheels. As the shadows deepened, a sudden feeling of terror descended upon both men, which was followed by an intense

BELOW: A 17th-century witch still returns to chill the blood of those who cross the wilder reaches of Enfield Chace.

feeling of hopeless melancholy. Moments later the horses shied and bolted without warning. The carriage was dragged forward at breakneck speed as Mr Ward struggled to control the terrified animals.

Suddenly, the moon burst from behind a bank of cloud and, as its yellow light illuminated the scene, both men saw the cause of the horses' alarm. Walking on the grass verge alongside them, and keeping up easily with the animals' speed, was a tall man with a deathly pale face. A deep, gaping wound ran along one side of his throat and glimmered in the moonlight.

On they galloped until, as they rounded a bend, the hideous spectre fell behind and stopped by a gate. The horses became calmer, their speed slackened. When the two men looked back, they saw the figure standing by the gate staring after them. As they watched, it began to fade and moments later it had vanished.

The next day Mr Ward recounted their experience to a friend and was astonished to learn that a man called Mr Danby had been murdered alongside that particular gate in 1832. Since then many people had encountered his spectre in the lane in which the crime occurred.

ENFIELD CHACE, EN4
The Witch of the Chace

The 17th century was a harsh and cruel time for those who lived around the desolate Enfield Chace. Plague was a frequent visitor, livestock died suddenly, crops failed and seemingly robust children perished under the onslaught of mysterious

ailments. But no matter what the tragedy, the local inhabitants were always convinced that witchcraft was responsible, and so they would attempt to flush out and punish a scapegoat. In 1622, one such supposed witch, who lived in an isolated hovel on the stretch of chace that is crossed by Hadley Road, was executed for witchcraft. Her spirit, however, has remained earthbound, for many is the person who has encountered the figure of a stooped and gnarled old hag, hobbling painfully along Hadley Road in the closing light of day.

ROSE AND CROWN
CLAY HILL, ENFIELD, EN2
Turpin Keeps on Riding

The ghost of the notorious 18th-century highwayman Dick Turpin must be one of the busiest in England! For that matter, with the number of pubs that claim his living self as a regular, it is a miracle he was ever able to remain upright in the saddle. Turpin's grandfather, one Mr Mott, once kept the Rose and Crown and local tradition maintains that the high-wayman often hid at the pub to evade capture. His ghost is said to haunt not only the pub but also the road outside, where Turpin gallops hell for leather through the night astride a jet black mount, no doubt en route to one of the many other pubs he is obliged to haunt before daybreak!

BELOW: Despite his legend, the real-life Dick Turpin was a vicious psychopath who would stop at nothing to get his way.

BELL LANE
ENFIELD, EN3
The Enfield Flyer

On a crisp December evening in 1961, young Robert Bird was cycling along Bell Lane on his way to a Boys' Brigade meeting, when he saw a pair of lights speeding towards him. As the lights came closer they suddenly swerved across the road and headed straight towards him. Convinced that an out-of-control vehicle was about to run him over, Robert attempted to move out of its path. But it was too late, and he braced himself for the inevitable impact. But the whole scene suddenly seemed to progress in slow motion, and Robert was able to observe that the vehicle was actually a black coach being pulled by four horses, all spurred on by two shadowy figures. However, strangest of all was the fact that the carriage was actually travelling several feet off the ground. Then, just as the coach was about to hit the boy, it passed straight through him and vanished.

This was the 'Phantom Coach of Enfield', a ghostly conveyance that races along Bell Lane with its wheels above the ground. Tradition holds that its origins lie in the 18th century, when the countryside in this area was marshland, and the road was a lot higher than it is today. It was quite common at the time for the speeding coaches to veer from the highway and plunge into the swampy surroundings, often with tragic results. Is it possible that this ghostly coach is a vestige of such a tragedy and has somehow left an imprint on its surroundings, which is occasionally re-enacted before startled spectators?

EAST LONDON

THE EAST OF LONDON might to be as overrun with ghosts as other parts of the capital, but the places where they choose to appear are certainly impressive and historic. Hackney's Sutton House is a place of creaking floorboards and shadowy corners and is everything a haunted house should be. Commercial Street's Ten Bells pub has changed little since the Jack-the-Ripper murders held the surrounding neighbourhood in a grip of steely terror. Head further east and you find yourself on the edge of Epping Forest, a vast and shaded expanse that boasts a few ghostly goings on beneath its shadowy canopy.

1. The Market Trader
2. The Ten Bells
3. Hanbury Street
4. The Bow Bells
5. Sutton House
6. Wanstead Park
7. St Mary the Virgin
8. The George, Wanstead
9. The George, South Woodford
10. St Paul's Church Pond
11. Chingford Mount Cemetery

THE MARKET TRADER
50 MIDDLESEX STREET, E1
The Ghosts of the Bell

The Market Trader pub stands on a busy corner overlooking Petticoat Lane street market. The building itself dates from the 18th century and was formerly called The Bell. Indeed a cursory glance upwards at the top gable reveals a bell in brick relief built into the exterior. Several people sitting in the upstairs bar have seen an old woman with long blonde hair and dressed in a white nightgown, walk to the corner and abruptly disappear. In 2003 a group of staff were watching television in one of the upstairs rooms when they heard footsteps walking along the corridor, followed by the sound of a door slamming shut. An assistant manager went to investigate, but could find no sign of anybody. He decided that, since he was in the pub, he

PREVIOUS PAGE: Eerie voices in the dead of night are just some of the supernatural phenomena to drift through Chingford Mount Cemetery.

BELOW: Jack the Ripper goes about his bloody business in the gas-lit streets of London's East End.

would go down to the kitchen and do some washing up. As he stood at the sink he heard a little girl giggling behind him and felt a light tap on his shoulder. Turning around he found he was alone. Thinking the other staff were playing a prank he raced upstairs and found them all still in the room. They swore that none of them had left the room. Lights that turn off of their own volition, and a ghostly couple that have been seen counting money in one of the bedrooms, are just some of the other strange occurrences that have been experienced at this historic and, in parts, spooky old East End Pub.

THE TEN BELLS
84 COMMERCIAL STREET, E1
Jack the Ripper's Local

The Ten Bells pub is indelibly linked with the legend of Jack the Ripper. Its interior, resplendent with a magnificent tiled wall panel depicting the days when this area was countryside outside the City of London, has hardly changed since the early hours of 9th November, 1888, when Mary Kelly, Jack the Ripper's final victim, left the pub. Her horrifically mutilated body was discovered next morning in Miller's Court, off Dorset Street on the opposite side of the road from The Ten Bells. Indeed, for many years in the 1970s and 1980s, the pub was renamed the Jack the Ripper, until, thanks largely to a landlord who was tastefully selling dark red 'Ripper Tipples', the brewery decided to return it to its original name in 1989.

In the late 1990s live-in staff, whose bedrooms were on the upper floors of the building, began to complain of alarming encounters with a ghostly old man dressed in Victorian clothing. They were often awoken by an uneasy feeling in the dead of night, and would find his phantom form lying beside them on the bed! As soon as they cried out in shock, the figure disappeared. Staff with no previous knowledge of his ghost would often report seeing him, and their descriptions would always be the same. Nobody had any idea who he was and those who had occasion to live on the premises, learnt to accept him as the pub's oldest resident.

In June 2000, however, a new landlord took over the pub and decided to clear out the cellar. He found an old metal box hidden away in a corner, and opening it, discovered it contained the personal effects of a man named George Roberts. The items dated from the early 1900s and with them was a brown leather wallet, inside which was a press cutting from the same period that talked of his having been murdered with an axe in a Swansea Cinema. Further research revealed that a man named George Roberts had indeed kept the pub in the late-19th and early-20th centuries and the landlord concluded that it was his ghost whom staff had been encountering.

A tenant who lived on the premises in 2001 often heard footsteps followed by a faint peal of laughter outside his door,

even when he was the only person on the premises. Whenever he investigated the sounds, he found the corridor outside empty. Going down into the bar to investigate further, he was often pushed hard on the back by an invisible hand.

A psychic was once brought to the pub to see what she could pick up on the premises. Having reached the top floor, she paused outside one of the rooms and refused to go any further. She said that she could sense that something terrible had happened in the room and was almost certain that it involved the brutal death of a baby in the 19th century. Lindsay Siviter, a leading researcher and expert on the Jack the Ripper crimes, was being shown around the pub a few years later and had been allowed access to the roof space. She noticed some material embedded in the floor behind the water tank and pulling at it found it was a sack tied at the top. Opening it she found it contained a mouldy set of Victorian baby clothes that appeared to have been slashed with a knife. Intriguingly the tank was directly above the room the psychic had refused to enter.

HANBURY STREET, E1
Jack the Ripper's Second Victim

The north side of Hanbury Street is now covered by the sprawling mass of the buildings that were formerly the Truman Brewery. It was built on the site of 29 Hanbury Street, in the back yard of which at around 6 a.m. on 8th September, 1888, the body of

ABOVE: Regulars at The Bow Bells can look forward to being flushed by the ghost!

Annie Chapman, Jack the Ripper's second victim, was discovered. In the days of the brewery it was often noticed that a strange chill drifted through the boardroom at 6 a.m. on the anniversary of the murder and it was also reported that Annie Chapman's ghost was sometimes seen standing by the wall of the storeroom that occupied the spot where she died.

THE BOW BELLS
116 BOW ROAD, E3
Flushed by the Ghost

The Bow Bells Pub stands on Mile End Road and has a down-at-heel ambience about it. Its ghost has the annoying – not to say alarming – habit of flushing the toilet in the ladies' as patrons happen to be sitting on it! In 1974, in a determined attempt to flush out the phantom responsible, the landlord decided to hold a séance. As the sitters gathered round and asked the spirit to make itself known, the toilet door suddenly swung open with such violence that a pane of its glass was shattered. Since then, successive landlords have grown used to sharing their pub with their phantom guest, who, in addition to his or her chain-pulling antics, sometimes appears as a translucent mist that oozes from the floor of the bar.

ABOVE: Not only is Sutton House one of London's oldest mansions, it is also one of the most haunted.

SUTTON HOUSE
2 & 4 HOMERTON HIGH STREET, E9
Howling Hounds and Shimmering Wraiths

The splendid red-brick Sutton House was built in 1535 by Sir Ralph Sadleir, one of Henry VIII's Privy Councillors. Since then it has been home to Huguenot silk-weavers, Victorian school-mistresses and Edwardian clergy. By the 1980s, the building had fallen into disrepair, its decline aided by squatters and vandals. Thankfully, due largely to the efforts of the Sutton House Community Scheme, the building was restored in the early 1990s and is now open to the public under the auspices of the National Trust. Although it has altered over the years, it remains essentially a Tudor house and its oak-panelled walls, grand staircase and carved fireplaces are reminiscent of a bygone age.

Needless to say, several ghosts wander its atmospheric interior. Dogs are heard wailing from the empty house in the dead of night. They are thought to be the dogs that belonged to John Machell, a wealthy wool merchant who lived at Sutton House from 1550 to 1558. Images of the dogs can still be seen in the coat of arms in the fireplace of the building's Little Chamber. Whenever dogs are brought into Sutton House, they often stop rigid at the foot of the painted staircase, their hackles raised, apparently transfixed by something they can see on the stairs but which remains invisible to humans. Another ghost is that of the White Lady, thought to be Frances, the wife of John Machell the younger. She died giving birth to twins on 11th May, 1574, and her shimmering shade has been seen gliding around the old rooms of the building. During the renovation of the property in the 1990s, an architectural student staying at the house, woke up in what is now the exhibition room, to find a lady in a blue dress hovering over his bed. A house steward recently encountered this same spectre when she rudely interrupted his slumbers by violently shaking his bed in the dead of night. Sudden drops in temperature, doors that open of their own accord and objects flung across rooms by unseen hands are just some of the other phenomena to be regularly encountered at this atmospheric old time-capsule.

WANSTEAD PARK, E11
Her Heart May Never Mend

Great Wanstead House is said to have been one of England's most spectacular stately homes, and once rivalled Blenheim Palace in its size and splendour. But when the last heiress to the estate, Lady Catherine Tylney, made an unwise marriage to a profligate nephew of the Duke of Wellington, its days of glory were numbered. He proceeded to gamble and drink away his wife's fortune and, in 1824, the couple were declared bankrupt. Their estate was seized and their house was pulled down and sold for building stone. Lady Catherine is said to have died of a broken heart when she discovered that her husband had been unfaithful to her. Her ghost has been seen drifting mournfully around the grounds of her former home and staring sadly into the ornamental pond in Wanstead Park.

ST MARY THE VIRGIN
OVERTON DRIVE, WANSTEAD, E11
Reunited After All These Years

A startling though poignant haunting has reputedly been witnessed in the churchyard that surrounds the 18th-century St Mary's Church. A skeleton, its bones bleached white, is said to cross the churchyard wheeling a coffin cart. As it approaches one of the tombs, a spectral wraith in a white shroud is said to rise from the earth and the two proceed to embrace one another. Witnesses, however, have nothing to fear, for the two are said to be a husband and wife who, for reasons unknown, were buried in separate parts of the churchyard, and now enjoy occasional ghostly reunions before startled spectators.

THE GEORGE
HIGH STREET, WANSTEAD, E11
Mad Mollie

A murder committed long ago and its tragic aftermath have apparently left their ethereal mark on the fabric of this otherwise pleasant Wanstead pub. The ghost is said to be that of 'Mad Mollie' a 19th-century barmaid who is said to have thrown her illegitimate child onto the pub's fire and then hanged herself from an upstairs beam. Although her body was cut down, it disappeared soon afterwards, and its whereabouts have never since been discovered. But her restless wraith returns to the bar of the pub where she wanders round in eternal remorse, a trapped entity doomed to contemplate her long ago act of ignominy for the whole of eternity.

THE GEORGE
GEORGE LANE, SOUTH WOODFORD, E18
The Infantile Footsteps

A spectral child is thought to be behind the ghostly goings on at this bustling and vibrant pub that stands at the end of a busy line of shops on South Woodford's main street. In the past items have been moved around, and childish footsteps have been heard running across rooms that are known to be empty. Legend holds that in the mid-19th century, a drunken landlord locked the unfortunate child in a cupboard in an alcohol-fuelled rage. The child suffocated in its airless prison and its ghost has haunted the pub ever since.

ST PAUL'S CHURCH POND
WOODFORD BRIDGE, E18
The Ghostly Orphans

The land hereabouts was once reputedly owned by Dr Barnardo's, and the churchyard apparently contained the graves of many orphaned children. This might be why people

ABOVE: Stand amidst the tumbledown graves at Chingford Mount Cemetery and a phantom on horseback might well gallop past.

walking near the pond have heard the ethereal sounds of children's laughter and singing, drifting through the air, even on the brightest of summer days.

CHINGFORD MOUNT CEMETERY
OLD CHURCH ROAD, E4
The Horseman Cometh

This vast necropolis, consisting mostly of Victorian graves, was once part of the estate of Lady Hamilton, the famed lover of Lord Nelson. Amongst its newer occupants are the infamous Kray twins, Ronnie and Reggie.

In 1971, the cemetery's superintendent reported that he and his wife had frequently been disturbed by 'eerie voices, whining noises and shaking sounds' in the dead of night. His son even witnessed a cloaked figure on a black horse cantering over the grass. More recently two women walking past the cemetery gates, heard voices whispering in conspiratorial tones 'fairly close by', although there was nobody else around at the time.

105

SOUTH-EAST LONDON

This varied chapter will take you to some truly mysterious places where former residents have been dying to meet you. Step into the charming George Inn, which is haunted by the ghost of a landlady who attempts to keep the contemporary world firmly at bay. Head down the Thames and a rich array of haunted buildings in the village of Greenwich will both delight and terrify.

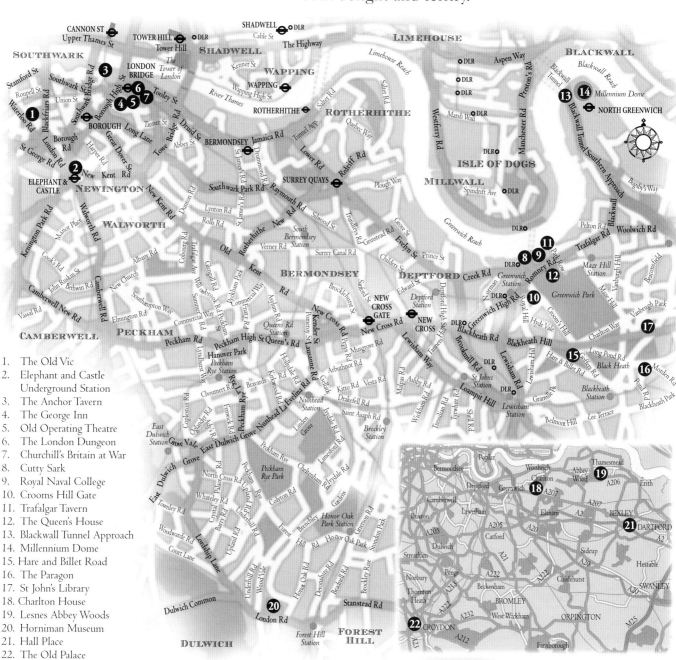

THE OLD VIC

THE OLD VIC
WATERLOO ROAD, SE1
The Bloodstained Spectre

Dating from the early part of the 19th century, and originally known as the Royal Coburg Theatre, The Old Vic was renamed the Royal Victoria Theatre in 1833, in honour of the young Princess Victoria. In 1912, Lillian Baylis became its manager and, over the next nine years, she set about raising its standards by staging new productions of all of Shakespeare's plays here. So successful was she that, by the end of World War I it had become one of London's leading theatres.

Over the years there have been several reports from startled witnesses of a spectral woman who has been seen in various parts of the theatre clasping her bloodstained hands to her breast. It is believed, but by no means proven, that the blood is actually make up, and that the revenant is an actress from a Shakespearean tragedy performed long ago, who, unwilling to take a final bow, feels compelled to repeat her ghostly encore over and over again.

ELEPHANT AND CASTLE UNDERGROUND STATION, SE17
The Passenger Who Never Leaves

Ghostly footsteps are often heard running through Elephant and Castle Station on storm-tossed winter's nights. Nobody knows what lies behind the phenomenon, but it has chilled the blood of many maintenance workers employed at the station during the night. A ghostly woman in dark clothing has also been observed getting onto trains, however, she has always disappeared by the next station.

THE ANCHOR TAVERN
34 PARK PLACE, SE1
The Mangy Old Dog Walks Again

Situated across the Thames from St Paul's Cathedral, this rambling 18th-century tavern was once a favourite watering hole of the writer Samuel Johnson (1709–84). It was also an infamous haunt of smugglers, who would hide their ill-gotten contraband in the secret rooms and cubby holes with which the pub is riddled. Here too came the notorious press-gangs, to cajole, bribe or even abduct 'volunteers' to crew the ships that sailed from the busy river port that London once was. Legend tells of one of their unfortunate conscripts who put up a great resistance to a gang of these recruitment special-

ists, as they tried to drag him, kicking and screaming, from the pub one night. The other customers, who averted their eyes, and gazed into their tankards, rather than risk attracting the attentions of the pressmen to themselves, politely ignored his cries. The man's dog, however, attempted a spirited defence of his master, and barked and snapped at the kidnappers, until one of the gang slammed the door shut with such force that it caught the animals tail and cut it clean off. The dog howled in pain and ran off into the night, never to be seen again.

Times have changed and the docks are long gone. Today it is tourists, not sailors, who come flocking to the old tavern from the far-flung reaches of the globe. The only press-gangs you are likely to encounter are groups of journalists from the nearby offices of the *Financial Times* and *Daily Express*. However, occasionally, as the clock ticks towards midnight, and staff are clearing away the detritus of another day's trading, the sound of a dog's paws padding along the corridors can be heard, and some staff claim to have seen the dejected shade of a mangy mutt wandering the pub, searching, so legend claims, for its severed tail!

THE GEORGE INN
77 BOROUGH HIGH STREET, SE1
The Formidable Phantom of Miss Murray

For centuries, Southwark's Borough High Street was lined with old Coaching Inns. 'Great rambling, queer old places,' according to Charles Dickens in The Pickwick Papers, '…with galleries, and passages, and staircases, wide enough and antiquated enough, to furnish materials for a hundred ghost stories…' Sadly, only one of them, The George Inn, survived the coming of the railways in the 19th century, and this little piece of bygone London now has the distinction of being the capital's only surviving galleried coaching inn.

The George Inn dates from 1677, and as you turn into its cobbled courtyard it is easy to imagine yourself transported back to another age. From the gallery that looks down upon the yard, long-forgotten travellers and inn workers once gazed upon the coaches as they clattered in through the gates below. You can almost hear the whinnying of the horses, the cursing of the stable hands and the banter of the coachmen. It, therefore, comes as little surprise to learn that this gem from London's past is haunted. Several members of staff residing on the premises have been woken in the early hours of some mornings to find the misty form of a woman floating around their rooms. Nobody knows for sure who she is, but a likely contender is the formidable

PREVIOUS PAGE: A ghostly actress covered in stage blood still treads the boards at the Old Vic.

BELOW: Step into Southwark's George Inn and you will feel you have been transported back in time. Just beware of the ghost.

Miss Murray, who kept the George for 50 years in the latter half of the 19th century and the early part of the 20th century. It was during her tenure that the coming of the railways sounded the death knell for the coaching age, and led to the demolition of the neighbouring inns. Three galleries of her beloved George were also demolished before public outcry succeeded in saving all that remained. Having watched so much of the property fall victim to the voracious appetite of the new age of horseless transport, Miss Murray's spirit possesses outright antagonism towards modern technology. New tills can be guaranteed to go wrong and engineers are called out time and again to repair them, but they can never find any logical explanation or genuine fault. Computers suddenly crash for no reason, and digital cameras have often malfunctioned when their owners have attempted to photograph the interior of what is, without doubt, one of London's most timeless hostelries.

It was at St Thomas's Hospital that Florence Nightingale (1820–1910) founded her school of nursing, and some think she might be one of the spirits that haunts the Old Operating Theatre. A photograph that had been taken of the museum interior was once displayed upon the wall, and many people claimed that they could see the apparition of a ghostly nurse standing in the background. Indeed, several people went so far as to insist that the image was unmistakably that of Florence Nightingale herself.

THE LONDON DUNGEON
28–34 TOOLEY STREET, SE1
A Ghostly Assault

In 1998 psychic investigator Paul Southcott, director of investigations for the grand-sounding 'Ufology and Supernatural Society', opted to spend a night in the London Dungeon armed with a video camera to investigate reports that the place was haunted. He discovered it to be 'teeming' with ghosts. Among the images that he caught on film were five ghostly faces that appeared through a brick wall, a spectral figure floating above the ground and a human skeleton in a gibbet cage that miraculously, and suddenly, began 'growing' flesh. 'The Jack the Ripper exhibits and the Judgement Day boat ride... were awash with paranormal activity,' he enthusiastically decreed.

Although the London Dungeon only moved to the site in 1975, the dank railway arches in which it is located date back to the 19th century. 'It's reported that part of the dungeon was once used as a prison,' explained Peter Armstrong the manager, 'and in the Second World War the arches were even employed as air-raid shelters.' Although Peter conceded that many of his staff believed the site to be haunted, he confessed to a healthy scepticism about the claims, maintaining that he took most of the stories he had heard 'with a large dose of salt'!

Meanwhile Paul Southcott discovered that at least one of the dungeon's spectres was not at all friendly. 'I was slapped in the face by a ghost in there,' he later told' the BBC World Service. 'It stung initially, then I felt sick and drained for days and suffered headaches.'

OLD OPERATING THEATRE
9A ST THOMAS'S STREET, SE1
Phantom Florence

Located in the unlikely setting of a church roof, and reached via a winding, wooden staircase that clings precariously to a wall, the Old Operating Theatre is without doubt one of London's most atmospheric and unique locations. Once used as the herb garret for nearby St Thomas's Hospital, it became its female operating theatre in 1822, and remained so until 1862 when it was sealed up and forgotten. Rediscovered in 1956, it was restored, and now functions as a medical museum. It is also let out for private parties at night, and staff working at these have come to terms with the fact that the place is haunted. Phantom footsteps have been heard running up the wooden staircase towards the storeroom, although when witnesses go to investigate there is never anyone there.

ABOVE: Marooned in dry dock at Greenwich the Cutty Sark is an eerie place to visit.

CHURCHILL'S BRITAIN AT WAR
64–66 TOOLEY STREET, SE1
The Phantom Sneeze

The Churchill's Britain at War exhibition occupies several railway arches over which trains trundle in and out of London Bridge Station. Its walls are hung with an evocative series of photographs and artefacts that depict the capital and its citizens facing the horrors of World War II. Several people have reported hearing a mysterious sneeze that seems to emanate from the corner of the lift through which the exhibition is entered, even though the corner in question remains empty. Others have heard a tuneless whistling echoing from deep within the displays.

CUTTY SARK
KING WILLIAM WALK, SE10
A Storm in a Bottle

Built in 1869 and once the fastest clipper ship of them all, the Cutty Sark now stands marooned on dry land, its splendid figurehead, intended as a good luck emblem to protect the ship and all who sailed in her, gazing dolefully towards the river. Many tales are told of sailors on board witnessing phantom ships in the days when the Cutty Sark plied its trade on the Australian wool route. Whenever they encountered such an apparition, the terrified sailors would scuttle to the figurehead

ABOVE: Elizabeth I is just one of several ghosts to haunt the magnificent buildings of the Royal Naval College, which is now home to Greenwich University.

a terrible storm blew up and whipped the sea into a foaming frenzy that pitched and tossed the Cutty Sark alarmingly. Suddenly, an enormous five-masted schooner appeared out of nowhere and hurtled towards the Cutty Sark. The crew rushed to the figurehead and cowered beneath it, waiting for the collision and its inevitable consequences. A huge wave crashed onto the deck and almost capsized the vessel. But when the ship righted itself, the phantom schooner had vanished. The sailors later learnt that, at the exact moment when the ghost ship had disappeared, their comrade had flung his model overboard into the raging ocean.

ROYAL NAVAL COLLEGE
ROMNEY ROAD, GREENWICH, SE10
Good Queen Bess and the Melancholic Admiral

The Royal Naval College, which is now part of Greenwich University, dates from the 17th century and stands on the site of Greenwich Palace, the birthplace of Henry VIII, Mary I and Elizabeth I. The palace was a favourite residence of Queen Elizabeth, and her ghost returns from time to time to wander the grounds and buildings that stand on the banks of the Thames. She wears a red wig and a low-necked period dress, but it is the small crown that adorns her hairpiece that has led to the conclusion that it is indeed the shade of the Virgin Queen.

Admiral John Byng (1704–57) haunts the rooms in Queen Anne block where he was confined prior to his execution for neglect of duty. His footsteps are heard pacing back and forth in the room in which he was imprisoned, and a shimmering apparition of him is often seen. The last occasion was on 15th June, 1993, when a security guard clearly saw him walk up the stairs of the Admiral President's block at 11 p.m.

and cower beneath it imploring its protection.

One day a mariner who was new to the ship whiled away his time by constructing a model of the Cutty Sark in a bottle. This seriously antagonized his crewmates who believed that such a recreation would bring about bad luck, and relations between the sailors on board became somewhat strained. Later

CROOMS HILL GATE
GREENWICH PARK, SE10
The Ancient Funeral Procession

In 1934, a woman walking her dog by Crooms Hill Gate in Greenwich Park was somewhat puzzled when the animal stopped in its tracks and, its hackles raised, began growling at something. Suddenly, she saw a procession of women, all of whom had reddish-brown hair, carrying a heavy coffin on their shoulders. Their legs stopped at the knees, giving the impression that they were 'wading through the earth as if through water'. She watched as the mysterious procession moved slowly towards the gate where, one by one, the ladies disappeared into thin air. The only explanation ever put forward to explain this strange manifestation is that, close to the gate, one can still discern a series of barrows. These were investigated in 1789 and deemed to be a female burial ground dating from the 5th and 6th centuries. Is it possible that what the lady saw was a spectral re-enactment of an ancient internment here, and that the raising of the ground since had resulted in their legs being cut off at the knees?

ABOVE: Did the Reverend Hardy photograph two ghosts on the Tulip Staircase of the Queen's House in 1966?

THE QUEEN'S HOUSE
ROMNEY ROAD, GREENWICH, SE10
Ghosts On Film?

Designed by Inigo Jones (1573–1652) for Charles I's wife, Henrietta Maria (1609–69), the Queen's House was completed in 1635 and is one of Greenwich's most elegant and graceful buildings. In 1966, the Reverend and Mrs R. W. Hardy, from White Rock, British Columbia, visited the house and took a photograph of its magnificent Tulip staircase. When they returned home and developed the film, a shrouded figure was clearly visible on this particular picture. Closer inspection revealed what appeared to be two figures, apparently ascending what had certainly been an empty staircase. Despite rigorous examination by photographic experts no rational explanation has ever been put forward to explain the presence of the figures, other than that they must have been there when the picture was taken.

TRAFALGAR TAVERN
5 PARK ROW, GREENWICH, SE10
The Ghostly Pianist

The Trafalgar Tavern was a favourite haunt of Charles Dickens, who came here to enjoy its famous whitebait dinners, which you can still do today – although the tasty little fish no longer come fresh from the River Thames. Staff maintain that there is a definite 'presence' at the pub, and that a decidedly icy chill sometimes hangs in the air. Some people have caught glimpses of a figure walking briskly across the upstairs rooms, although when they take a closer look there is nobody there. Other phenomena includes beer crates being lifted into the air by invisible hands in the pub cellar and the figure of a man in Victorian dress who has been seen sitting by the upstairs piano.

BLACKWALL TUNNEL
APPROACH, SE10
The Phantom Hitchhiker

Phantom hitchhikers are a popular, though dubious, part of modern international ghost lore. Indeed, their tales follow an established and common pattern that is amply illustrated by this tale from the Blackwall Tunnel. In October 1972 a motorcyclist stopped to give a lift to a male hitchhiker on the Greenwich approach to the tunnel. The two managed to hold a conversation, during which the man told the driver where he lived. As their conversation was drowned out by the noise of the traffic, the motorcyclist concentrated on the road. On arrival at the other side, he was astonished to find that his passenger had disappeared. Alarmed and mystified he drove through the tunnel a few times, but could find no sign of the stranger. The next day he went round to the address that the man had supplied him with. There he gave his description of the hitchhiker, only to discover that it matched that of a son of the family who had been killed in the tunnel while riding pillion on a motorcycle several years earlier.

MILLENNIUM DOME, SE10
The Prophetic Laughing Phantom

The offices of the South Metropolitan Gas Works, which formerly occupied the site of the Millennium Dome, were long rumoured to be haunted. It was widely believed that the bearded phantom, which put in regular appearances to disrupt the working day of the staff by messing up their desks, was that of Sir George Livesey, the company's former chairman. In life, Livesey had been a philanthropic and popular employer who had, amongst other things, introduced a profit-sharing scheme for his workers. When he died at the ripe old age of 90 years, 7,000 people turned out to pay their last respects at his funeral. However, his spirit seems to have been loath to depart from the site where he had spent so much of his working life. When the gas works closed down Livesey was often seen wandering around the derelict buildings. His spectral activity intensified when work began to clear the ground for the construction of the Millennium Dome. On many occasions builders looked up from their tasks to find Livesey's distinguished figure watching them. After a few moments of incredulous gazing, his face would crack into a grin and he would let out a peal of chuckling laughter. Spokespeople for the Millennium project were forced to confess total bafflement as to what could be causing the spectre such obvious merriment!

> '**HIS LUSTFUL GHOST ROAMS THE CORRIDORS AND PASSAGES OF CHARLTON HOUSE IN SEARCH OF LIVING LADIES THAT TAKE HIS FANCY...**'
>
> THE LECHEROUS WRAITH OF SIR WILLIAM LANGHOME

HARE AND BILLET ROAD
BLACKHEATH, SE3
She Awaits Her Lover

A doomed love affair and its tragic consequences are thought to lie behind the spectre that walks its doleful path along Hare and Billet Road. In the latter half of the 19th century a Greenwich woman of high birth is said to have fallen in love with a married man. One day he promised her faithfully that he was about to leave his wife, and asked his lover to meet him by a great elm that then stood along a bleak and desolate stretch of Blackheath. But he never came, and the disconsolate lady hanged herself from one of the branches of the tree. Since then, her forlorn phantom has been seen on many occasions, pacing fretfully back and forth along Hare and Billet Road, wringing her hands in despair, and hoping beyond hope, that her fickle lover will one day appear.

THE PARAGON
BLACKHEATH, SE3
The Ghostly Maid Is Seen No More

The elegant houses that curve gracefully around the crescent of The Paragon in Blackheath date from 1794, although they were restored between 1947 and 1957, following bomb damage sustained during World War II. Many years have passed since the ghostly white lady was seen here. However, should she ever choose to glide around the crescent again, it is worth noting that local tradition maintains that she is the ghost of a maidservant called Annie Hawkins, who drowned herself in a nearby pond following an unhappy love affair.

ST JOHN'S LIBRARY
BLACKHEATH, SE3
Elsie Marshall's Poignant Shade

Formerly the vicarage of St John's Church, this site was the childhood home of Elsie Marshall, whose father became vicar in 1874. Elsie became a missionary and travelled to China in 1892 to spread the good word in a remote province. Her cheerful and patient countenance inspired all who met her. But on 1st August, 1895, a gang of bandits attacked the mission

and slaughtered everyone, including Elsie. Her spirit, however, journeyed back to the vicarage in which she had grown up, and continues to haunt the library that now occupies the building. Staff are actually quite fond of Elsie's ghost, and since she harms no one, they are content to just let her be. She makes her presence known in a variety of ways, including switching on the lights when the building is empty at night. Some visitors to the library have felt her unseen presence brush by them at the entrance, whilst others have felt the cold touch of her fingers stroking the backs of their necks. However, when staff inform them that they have felt the ghost of Elsie Marshall, they leave happy, honoured to have been singled out for her phantom attention.

ABOVE: Beware the amorous apparition of Charlton House, for he may well still be intent on begetting an heir.

CHARLTON HOUSE
CHARLTON ROAD, SE7
The Amorous Spectre

Charlton House was built between 1607 and 1612 for Sir Adam Newton, Dean of Durham and tutor to Prince Henry, son of James I. It is little short of a Jacobean statement in architecture and, as such, is one of the finest and best-preserved mansions of that era in London. When Newton died it passed to his son, Henry, and via successive owners, it came into the possession of the wealthy East India Merchant, Sir William Langhorne. He may have been exceedingly rich, but Langhorne's fortune could do nothing to grant his dearest wish, that of begetting an heir. As he grew to old age he became increasingly distressed that he had no children, and when his first wife died, undeterred by the fact that he was in his 80s, in 1715, he took a second bride who was aged just 17. But when he died two months later, his young wife had not conceived, and thus the house passed through a number of different hands before coming into the possession of the Maryon-Wilson family who owned it from 1767 to 1923.

But Sir William Langhorne has proved both unable and unwilling to depart from the house, and his determination to beget an heir has continued beyond the grave. Thus his lustful ghost roams the corridors and passages of Charlton House in search of living ladies that take his fancy. In the past, many women staying at the house were awoken by the alarming sound of their bedroom door handles turning in the dead of night. Those brave enough to investigate would throw open the door only to find the corridor outside dark and empty. Occasionally women walking down the stairs have had their bottoms pinched by Langhorne's amorous, though invisible, fingers.

BELOW: Every appearance of the Black Prince's phantom at Hall Place is said to bring England bad luck.

During World War I Charlton House was converted into a Military Hospital and the owner, Lady Spencer Maryon-Wilson, informed the nursing staff that they were on no account to put patients in one particular bedroom, which had the reputation of being haunted. Unfortunately as casualties increased, her wishes had to be ignored and several of the wounded placed in the room claimed to have encountered its resident wraith.

In 1925 the house was purchased by the Metropolitan Borough of Greenwich and subsequently used as a community centre and library. In World War II the north wing was destroyed by bombing and, in the course of later restoration work, the mummified body of an infant was found concealed in one of its chimneys. Nobody could discover the baby's identity, or the reason why it had been hidden there, but the grisly discovery may explain the sightings of a ghostly servant girl in old-fashioned clothing seen walking about the grounds with a dead baby cradled in her arms.

LESNES ABBEY WOODS, SE2
The Phantom Vanishes

Lesnes Abbey was founded in 1178 by Richard de Luci as an act of penance for supporting King Henry II in the dispute with Archbishop Thomas à Becket, a row that resulted in the holy man's murder. The abbey was suppressed by Cardinal Wolsey in 1525, and, having passed through several hands, it came into the possession of Christ's Hospital and was taken over by the London County Council in 1930. Consisting of over 200 acres of woodland, carpeted in spring by a rich profusion of daffodils and bluebells, Lesnes Abbey now forms one of London's loveliest open spaces. The abbey ruins were excavated in 1909, and this may have disturbed the revenant of one of the long-dead monks, for several people have reported catching ethereal glimpses of a hooded figure flitting around the woods, which abruptly vanishes if they look at it full on.

HORNIMAN MUSEUM
LONDON ROAD, FOREST HILL, SE23
The Dancing Phantoms

In the 1860s, Victorian tea trader Frederick Horniman began collecting specimens and artefacts from around the globe with the express intention of bringing the wider world to Forest Hill. To that end, in 1890, he began opening his house to the public three times a week. In 1898 Horniman's house was demolished and Charles Harrison Townsend constructed a new museum in the Art Nouveau style. The museum opened in 1901, and was granted as a gift to the people of London in perpetuity for their recreation and their enjoyment. The museum is still thriving and is a wonderful place to visit.

Visitors may also have the opportunity of making the acquaintances of the ghostly man and woman that haunt the terrace to the side of the conservatory at the rear of the museum. Nobody knows for certain who they are, although there is general consensus from witnesses that they are dressed in the fashions of the 1920s. The man's hair is heavily greased back, while the woman's most notable feature is the bright red dress that she wears. They appear to be enjoying a distant garden party or ball, for those who encounter them are emphatic that they are dancing across the terrace, although no music is ever heard. After a few moments, the waltzing wraiths spin their way into the trees and are gone!

ABOVE: The ghostly party at the Horniman Museum is so enjoyable that two of its guest are loath to leave.

HALL PLACE
BOURNE ROAD, BEXLEY, KENT, DA5
The Black Prince

This flint and brick Tudor house with 17th-century additions, is named for the 13th-century owners of the property, the At-Halls. In 1356, it was from this house that Edward III's oldest son, the Black Prince (1330–76), set off to fight in the French campaign. His phantom still appears at the property, although its manifestations are said to be a bad omen for the fortunes of England. Clad in black armour, his figure is said to have appeared three times prior to British setbacks in World War II.

Hall Place's second ghost is said to be that of Lady Constance At-Hall, who had the misfortune of witnessing her husband, Sir Thomas, being gored to death by a stag in front of her. In her despair she is said to have flung herself to her death from the building's tower. Her pitiful moans have been heard about the property, and mysterious footsteps, accompanied by strange tapping, have also been heard in the dead of night. From time to time, a shadowy figure has been seen gazing forlornly from the tower. In the 1950s a medium visited the house and established that a servant girl who suffered personal tragedy at the house causes some of the phenomena. Her ghost has since been seen several times in one of the attic bedrooms.

THE OLD PALACE
CROYDON, CR0
The Wringing Spectre

Now a school, the Old Palace in Croydon was formerly the home of successive Archbishops of Canterbury, the medieval lords of the manor. It was visited by many illustrious figures, including Henry III, Edward I, Henry IV, Henry VII, Henry VIII, Mary I and Elizabeth I. The see of Canterbury relinquished ownership of the site in 1758, and the building later became an orphanage. It is the ghost of the mother of one of the 19th-century orphans that is said to haunt the building. She appears terribly sad, wringing her hands in grief as she roams the rooms in an eternal search for her lost child.

SOUTH-WEST LONDON

MOVING TO THE SOUTH-WEST SUBURBS of London, haunted sites become a little thin on the ground. But what the buildings here lack in quantity is more than made up for by the quality of the ghosts that wander their shadows. From the wives of Henry VIII that haunt Hampton Court Palace, to the ghostly Cavalier that gallops across Richmond park, the phantoms of this area are amongst the most illustrious in London. Finally, there is the strange story of the ghostly re-enactment of a car crash, which led the police to the hidden wreckage of a very real car crash at that very spot.

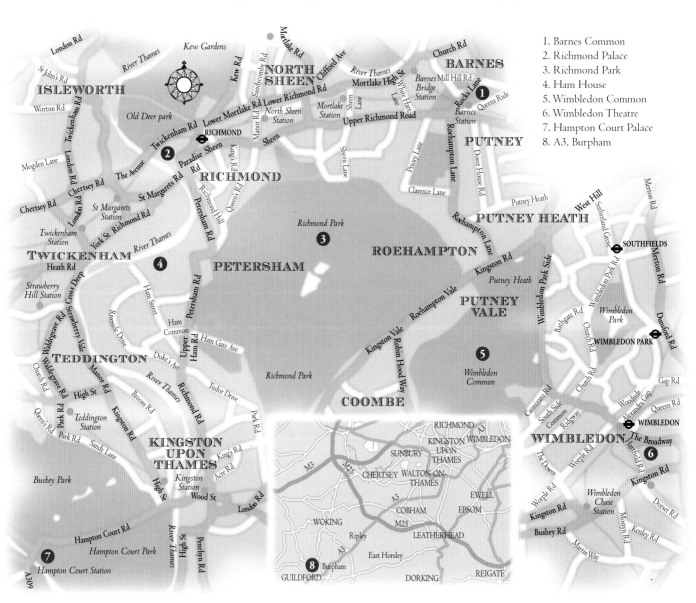

1. Barnes Common
2. Richmond Palace
3. Richmond Park
4. Ham House
5. Wimbledon Common
6. Wimbledon Theatre
7. Hampton Court Palace
8. A3, Burpham

ABOVE: In the 19th century those crossing, or even living around, Barnes Common were in danger of being attacked by Spring Heel Jack.

PREVIOUS PAGE: Richmond Palace's Gatehouse. Did Elizabeth I's ghost take a stroll through Richmond Palace at the moment of her death?

BARNES COMMON
COMMON ROAD, SW13
The Exploits of Spring Heel Jack

Little now remains of the original Barnes Common, which in 1838 was one of the haunts of the mysterious and terrifying figure known as 'Spring Heel Jack'. The spirit would bound towards the common from the vicinity of the old churchyard, his appearance 'hideous and frightful… vomiting blue and white flame from his mouth', and attack lone travellers crossing the common at night. However, after a short reign of terror, his appearances ceased.

Today a man in grey clothes, that some say resemble a prison uniform, is the sole ghostly occupant of Barnes Common. He glides furtively about, looking as though he is about to commit some dastardly crime, but when challenged

he melts away before astonished witnesses. One theory is that he is the ghost of a 19th-century convict, who having managed to escape from nearby Putney Hospital, froze to death on Barnes Common.

RICHMOND PALACE
THE GREEN, RICHMOND, TW9
The Death of the Virgin Queen

In January 1603, acting upon the advice of her astrologer, Dr John Dee, Elizabeth I left Whitehall Palace and headed up river to Richmond. Apart from a courtyard and red-brick gatehouse, little now survives of Richmond Palace, but in 1603 it was known as the queen's 'warm winter box'. Shortly after her arrival, Elizabeth was plunged into depression by word of the death of her cousin and close friend, the Countess of Nottingham. Then, in early March, she came down with a severe chill, which turned to pneumonia. Despite it being apparent to all around her that the she was seriously ill, Elizabeth refused to take to her bed. 'If you were in the habit of seeing such things in your bed as I do in mine,' she told her concerned advisers, 'you would not persuade me to go there.' By the 21st March, 1603, it was obvious that the queen was dying, and only then did she retire to her bed.

At around 10 p.m. on the night of 23rd March, Elizabeth sighed, turned her face to the wall and sank into a deep sleep. As she did so, one of her ladies-in-waiting left the room to return briefly to her own quarters. Walking down one of the palace's gloomy corridors, she was astonished to meet Elizabeth's unmistakable figure striding towards her. She looked round to see if anyone else was in the corridor and when she looked back the figure had vanished. Wondering if the queen had made a miraculous recovery, she raced back to the royal bedchamber, but found the monarch still unconscious. Is it possible that, as the last Tudor monarch clung to life, her spirit had left her body and taken a final stroll through Richmond Palace?

RICHMOND PARK
RICHMOND
The Ghostly Cavalier

The 2,470 acres that comprise Richmond Park were first enclosed in 1637 by Charles I to enlarge the grounds of Richmond Palace. Following his execution in 1649, the Commonwealth government gave the park to the City of London in return for its support during the Civil War. With the Restoration of the monarchy under Charles II, the City returned the land to the Crown. Today it is a delightful place to wander and take the air, and the profusion of wildlife to which the park is home include, hares, rabbits and herds of deer that graze lazily beneath the towering trees. It is also home to a ghost whose origins may well date back to the dark days of the Civil War when England was divided between the Royalists and the Parliamentarians. In May and June 2003 there were reports of nebulous encounters with a ghostly cavalier amidst the foliage of the park. Some people who were walking in the park late in the afternoon spoke of catching fleeting glimpses of this spectral figure. One witness told how he seemed quite solid when spied from afar but spoke of how, as she got closer to him, he became almost transparent before disappearing into thin air.

HAM HOUSE
HAM STREET, HAM, RICHMOND, TW10
The Searching Spectre

Known as the 'sleeping beauty' of country houses this splendid building has changed little since the 17th century. Built as a modest country residence by Sir Thomas Vavasour in 1610, the house was acquired by William Murray, 1st Earl of Dysart in 1637. Vavasour was a nobleman who had enjoyed the enviable position of whipping boy to the future Charles I as a youth. Chief amongst his duties was that he should be punished for the prince's misbehaviour!

In 1651 Murray bequeathed the house to his daughter, Elizabeth, Countess of Dysart, the wife of Sir Lyonel Tollemache by whom she had 11 children. Rumours were rife that she was also the mistress of Oliver Cromwell who, gossip maintained, was the father of her second son, Thomas. After the Restoration, she became the lover of the Duke of Lauderdale, marrying him in 1672, following the death of Sir Lyonel.

An intriguing tale tells of the six-year-old daughter of a 19th-century butler at Ham House who was invited by the then owners, the Ladies Tollemache, to come and stay at the property. In the early hours of the morning, the girl awoke to find a little old lady scratching upon the wall by the fireplace with her fingers. Sitting up to get a better view of the stranger, she seemed to disturb the woman who came to the foot of the bed and proceeded to stare at the child with a fixed and horrible gaze. This sent the child into screaming hysterics, alerting other members of the household who came racing to the room. They could find no sign of the old woman but, on searching the wall, they uncovered a secret compartment. Within this they uncovered papers which proved the Countess of Dysart had murdered her first husband in order that she might marry the Duke of Lauderdale.

ABOVE: Elizabeth I died at Richmond Palace, her 'warm winter box'. Her doppelgänger was seen there shortly before her death.

WIMBLEDON COMMON
WIMBLEDON, SW19
Wild and Windswept

The 1,100 unenclosed acres of Wimbledon Common are lonely and desolate in parts, and several wanderers have reported alarming encounters with its ghostly inhabitants while wending their way through the thickets and undergrowth. The actor Edward Silward, whom, we are told, was famed in the first half of the 20th century for his 'extremely clever impersonation of a gorilla', was crossing the common alone one night, when a man in convicts' clothing ran across the ground directly in front of him and promptly disappeared. When discussing the matter with friends, Silward learnt that many others had encountered a similar apparition around the common. To this day, people still speak of catching glimpses of a grey figure running across the turf, which has vanished when they attempt to look at it more closely.

WIMBLEDON THEATRE
BROADWAY, SW19
The Cackling Phantom

The Wimbledon Theatre opened on 26th December, 1910, with the pantomime *Jack and Jill*, beginning a tradition of family Christmas shows at the venue that has continued ever since. The original manager of the theatre was the impresario J. B. Mullholland, and his ghostly form has made fleeting returns from time to time to sit in one of the boxes, where he is happy to oversee rehearsals, or to simply watch the play being performed on the stage.

Far more active is the 'Grey Lady', who appeared in the bedroom of the manageress in 1980 as just a head and torso. The macabre spectre proceeded to ascend to the ceiling, let out a loud, raucous cackle, and vanish into the fabric. Elsewhere, stagehands and usherettes have seen her misty form, sometimes sitting in the front row of the gallery, and at other times passing through closed doors. On one occasion the ghost was even spotted strolling contentedly out of the Ladies' toilet!

The Grey Lady also has the annoying habit of switching on the theatre's sprinkler system. When this last occurred, the safety curtain was quickly lowered to prevent the orchestra pit from flooding. However, staff were most surprised to discover that, although the water had got into the orchestra pit, the safety curtain itself had somehow managed to remain completely dry.

ABOVE: The ghosts of Kings and Queens, Lords and Ladies vie for your attention at Hampton Court Palace.

OPPOSITE: Catherine Howard the fourth wife of Henry VII is the most dramatic of Hampton Court's ghosts.

In the 18th century the common was a notorious haunt of footpads (robbers) and highwaymen who were only too willing to relieve travellers of their possessions and even their lives. One of the most infamous was Jerry Abershaw, who was finally brought to justice in 1795. After his execution his body was hung on a gibbet and placed on Wimbledon Hill to act as a deterrent to others who might be planning similar transgressions. Today his ghost is said to gallop across the common at great speed, the dull thud of his phantom mount's hooves clearly audible as the two ride into the night and vanish.

HAMPTON COURT PALACE
EAST MOLESEY, KT8
Royal Revenants

In 1529, Cardinal Wolsey constructed a magnificent palace on the banks of the Thames. He lived in the completed building in regal splendour and entertained on such a lavish scale that his hospitality became the talk of Europe. But, when he failed in his attempts to persuade the Pope to annul the marriage of Henry VIII and Katharine of Aragon, his fate and downfall were sealed. In a last desperate attempt to buy his way back into Royal favour, the crestfallen cardinal presented his 'jewel on the

Thames' to Henry, who gratefully accepted the gift and then promptly summoned Wolsey to answer charges of treason. Frail in both mind and body, the dejected cleric headed south from his see at York, but died en route at Leicester, wishing that he had 'served God as diligently as I have served my King'.

Henry wasted no time in introducing his second wife, Anne Boleyn, to the splendours of Wolsey's Palace and, following her beheading in 1536, her ghost remained behind to drift forlornly through its passages and chambers wearing a blue dress. Typically, Henry was courting Jane Seymour (c.1509–37) while Anne was still alive. She became his third wife, and she did seem to bring the despotic tyrant genuine contentment, providing him with his longed-for son and heir, Edward, who was born on 12th October, 1537. Sadly, shortly afterwards, Jane Seymour died (from natural causes) and ever since her phantom has made an annual pilgrimage to the palace, on the anniversary of her son's birth. Holding an unflickering candle, her head bent in sorrow, she glides eerily along corridors, passes through closed doors and has, on occasion, shocked witnesses into resigning from the palace's staff.

But it is Henry's fifth wife Catherine Howard, who makes the most dramatic return to Hampton Court Palace. She was still a teenager when she married the King in 1540, although she was certainly sexually experienced. Her past liaisons had included her music master, Henry Mannock, and a youthful nobleman named Dereham. She found Henry physically repulsive and had soon sought solace in the arms of a young man at court, Thomas Culpeper. Servants' tittle-tattle brought her previous indiscretions to light and, not long afterwards, her adultery was exposed. Henry was furious at the betrayal. The unfortunate Culpeper was soon languishing in the Tower of London and was subsequently executed (as was Mannock), and his unfaithful queen found herself imprisoned in her chambers at Hampton Court. Brooding on her inevitable fate, the young girl decided that her only hope lay in meeting with her husband, and pleading with him to spare her life. On 4th November, 1541, knowing that Henry would be at prayer in the chapel, she broke free from her guards and ran through what is now known as the 'Haunted Gallery' where she threw herself at the chapel's locked door, screaming at her husband to grant her an audience. Henry listened in stony silence and, moments later the guards had recaptured the hysterical girl and were dragging her back to her chambers. On 13th February, 1542, at just 20 years of age, Catherine Howard went bravely to the block with the words: 'I die a Queen but I had rather died the simple wife of Tom Culpeper. May God have mercy on my soul. Pray for me.' She was smiling when the axe fell. Ever since, servants, noblemen and even modern-day wardens have reported seeing her ghost, dressed in a white gown, racing towards the chapel, her face contorted into a terrifying, unearthly scream. Many visitors have reported a peculiar, icy coldness and intense feeling of desperate sadness around the doors of the chapel itself, and some people have even witnessed a disembodied, ringed hand knocking upon the door. As recently as 1999 two women on separate guided tours fainted at exactly the same spot in the 'Haunted Gallery'. On regaining consciousness, both victims reported a sudden chill and said they felt as if they had been punched shortly before passing out.

Hampton Court has more than thirty ghosts residing within its ancient fabric. History certainly does come alive here and to explore its fascinating rooms and passages is to walk with kings and queens, lords and ladies, the famous and forgotten.

A3, BURPHAM
NEAR GUILDFORD, SURREY
A Ghostly Replay?

On Wednesday, 11th December, 2002, Surrey Police received several calls from motorists to say that a car had veered off the A3 with its headlights blazing. However, when officers arrived at the scene they could find no sign of a crashed vehicle, and it appeared to have vanished without trace. A further search was ordered – and the results were chilling. For, just 20 yards from the supposed 'crash scene', police found the wreckage of a car containing the remains of a man, buried in twisted undergrowth. Its lights were off – the battery had long since died – and the body was little more than a skeleton. Surrey Police later revealed that the crash had, in fact, happened in July 2002, and that the vehicle had lain undiscovered for nearly five months. The motorists who had originally alerted the police were therefore left to ponder the eerie possibility that what they had seen was a ghostly re-enactment of the original accident.

FURTHER READING

Abbott, Geoffrey *Ghosts of the Tower of London*,
　Heinemann, 1980

Alexander, Marc *Phantom Britain*, Muller, 1975

Barker, Felix & Silvester-Carr, Denise *The Black Plaque Guide
　to London*, Constable, 1987

Brooks, J. A *Ghosts of London*, Jarrold, 1993

Byrne, Thomas *Tales From the Past*, Ironmarket, 1977

Coxe, Anthony D. Hippisley, *Haunted Britain*, Pan, 1975

Green, Andrew *Our Haunted Kingdom*,
　Fontana/Collins, 1973

Hallam, Jack *The Haunted Inns of England*, Wolfe, 1972

Harper, Charles *Haunted Houses*, Bracken, 1993

Jones, Richard *Walking Haunted London*, New Holland, 1999

Jones, Richard *Haunted Britain and Ireland*,
　New Holland, 2001

Jones, Richard *Myths and Legends of Britain and Ireland*,
　New Holland, 2003

Jones, Richard *Haunted Castles of Britain and Ireland*,
　New Holland, 2003

Jones, Richard *Haunted Inns of Britain and Ireland*,
　New Holland, 2004

Jones, Richard *Walking Dickensian London*,
　New Holland, 2004

Marsden, Simon, *The Haunted Realm*, Little, Brown, 1986

Mason, John *Haunted Heritage*, Collins and Brown, 1999

McEwan, Graham J. *Haunted Churches of England*,
　Robert Hale, 1989

Murphy, Ruth & Whicelow, Clive *Mysterious Wimbledon*,
　Enigma, 1994

Playfair, Guy Lion *The Haunted Pub Guide*, Javelin, 1987

Puttick, Betty *Ghosts of Essex*, Countryside, 1997

Reader's Digest, *Folklore, Myths and Legends of Britain*,
　Reader's Digest Association Limited, 1977

Underwood, Peter *This Haunted Isle*, Javelin, 1986

Weinrob, Ben & Hibbert, Christopher (editors) *The London
　Encylopedia*, Macmillan, 1993

INDEX